JEET KUNE DO
EQUIPMENT TRAINING

By CHRIS KENT

DISCLAIMER: Please note that the author and publisher of this book are NOT RESPONSIBLE in any manner whatsoever for any injury that may result from practicing the techniques and/or following the instructions given within. Since the physical activities described herein may be too strenuous in nature for some readers to engage in safely, it is essential that a physician be consulted prior to training.

First published in 2020 by AWP LLC/Empire Books.

Copyright © 2020 AWP LLC/Empire Books. All rights reserved.

No part of this publication may be reproduced or utilized in any form or by any means, electronic or mechanical, including photo- copying, recording, or by any information storage and retrieval system, without prior written permission from AWP LLC/Empire Books.

EMPIRE BOOKS
P.O. Box 491788, Los Angeles, CA 90049

First edition: Library of Congress Catalog Number:
ISBN-13: 978-1-949753-27-1

20 19 18 17 16 15 14 13 12 11 10

Library of Congress Cataloging-in-Publication Data:
Jeet Kune Do -- Guide to Equipment Training / by Chris Kent. -- 1st ed. p. cm. Includes index.

ISBN 978-1-949753-27-1 (pbk.: alk. paper) 1. Jeet Kune Do. 5. Martial Arts -- Interviews. 3. Large type books. I. Title. GV1332.3.F715 2014   769.815'3 -- dc24   ·   2006014423

PRINTED IN THE UNITED STATES OF AMERICA

DEDICATION

To my wife, Leslie, and our daughter, Sarah Leilani -- the two people who make it all worthwhile.

Mahalo nui lo.

ACKNOWLEDGEMENTS

Thanks to the following people for their assistance in the making of this book:

John Bunch

John has been a private student and training partner of Chris Kent for over 19 years. He is a certified, full Instructor in Jeet Kune Do and currently serves a member of the Kent Institute of Martial Art's instructor staff.

Rik Hinton

Rik has trained in JKD for over 17 years and is a certified Full Instructor in Jeet Kune Do. He currently serves as a member of the Kent Institute of Martial Arts instructor staff. Special thanks to Rik for shooting the additional photographs for the book.

I would also like to thank:

Jose M. Fraguas – For his dedication and commitment as a publisher to creating high quality books, publications, and DVDs.

Cass Magda – My close friend and JKD brother, for sharing his knowledge and expertise as we walked the JKD and Filipino martial art path.

John Little – My good friend, for helping me develop into a better writer and communicator, and for the numerous in-depth discussions we have shared over the years on all matters to do with JKD.

TABLE OF CONTENTS

Introduction   1

Mobile Equipment

Chapter 1: *Focus Gloves*   6

Chapter 2: *Kicking Shield*   129

Chapter 3: *Forearm Pads*   171

Fixed Equipment

Chapter 4: *The Heavy Bag*   219

Chapter 5: *Double-end Bag*   275

Chapter 6: *Wall Bag, Paper Target and Plastic Ball*   291

Chapter 7: *The Wooden Dummy*   299

Chapter 8: *Training with Body Protective Equipment*   333

Appendix A: *Achieving Personal Martial Art Excellence, and More*   342

Article: *JKD – An Art Caught in an Identity Crisis*   351

INTRODUCTION

Developing Your Martial "Instrument"

As a martial artist, your body is the "instrument" you use to communicate with in combative form. And the more finely tuned your instrument, the higher degree of efficiency and effectiveness it can express, and the greater your ability to move your body and adapt instantly and harmoniously to whatever type of opponent happens to be in front of you will be. While your entire body is the martial instrument, the various elements used in striking such as your hands, feet, elbows, knees, and even head, make up what are often referred to as the combative "tools of the trade." Each of these various combative tools needs to be developed, maintained and/or sharpened on a daily basis in order to be kept in perfect working order and be most efficient and effective. A proficient martial artist must possess the ability to relate their various strikes to an opponent as part of an intuitive arsenal, and develop the ability to strike from any distance, at every angle and with either arm or leg to take advantage of the moment. To help facilitate this, the continual development and refinement of the various striking tools should make up a significant portion of your training regimen. You should train every part of your body so that when you need a particular tool you can call upon it at will and it's instantly there. When you want to punch or kick, you <u>are</u> punching or kicking. And that punch or kick has totality, speed, agility, power, flexibility and accuracy. In other words, you've trained yourself to become one with it -- the tool is an extension of you.

The Importance of Training with Equipment

Realistic impact training on equipment is a vital and necessary training component for any martial artist seeking to develop or enhance their performance skills. Training with equipment is essential in improving the proficiency of any athlete. Can you imagine a basketball player practicing without a ball and hoop? Or a hockey player without his stick and a puck, simply going through the motions he plans to use in a game? The practice of such things as visualization exercises and shadowboxing, while useful training tools, will only take you so far. As a martial artist, how can you expect to understand what it feels like to really land a strike on an opponent if you've never hit anything? Can you imagine today's mixed martial art champions relying strictly on using their imagination to develop such qualities as speed, power, accuracy and timing in their striking skills?

The late Bruce Lee was a pioneer in the development and use of much of the equipment we see being used on a daily basis in the field of martial art training today. In an era when the vast majority of martial artists spent the majority of their time practicing pre-rehearsed 'katas' or forms, punching and kicking air, and concentrating on breaking boards and bricks, Lee, in contrast, took a scientific approach to not only martial art, but also training for it. A firm believer in the necessity of utilizing training equipment to enhance personal development, Lee used a widely varied assortment of training devices to sharpen and maintain his combative tools. Some of this equipment, such as the heavy bag, the top-and-bottom (double-end) bag, and the wall bag, he could use by himself. Other equipment, such as the focus gloves, kicking shield, and forearm pads, required a training partner. Certain specialized pieces of equipment such as the Mook Jong (Wooden Dummy) were used not only for training specific combative elements, but also because a human training partner simply couldn't withstand the continued force and power dealt out for hundreds of repetitions during one of Lee's training sessions. However, each piece of equipment served as an integral part in Lee's overall training program.

Equipment training allows you to explore your own capabilities and actualize your true potential as a martial artist. It helps you discover your strengths and is also invaluable for developing areas in which you're weak or deficient. The use of various types of training equipment allows you to cover the entire spectrum of training and can be used to develop not only various technical actions, such as a particular kick or strike, but also to improve or enhance certain qualities such as speed, power, timing, distance, rhythm, etc. You can use equipment to develop non-detectable and non-rhythmic movement, or to enhance your auditory and visual response to an opponent's motion. Various pieces of equipment may be used to develop different aspects of one particular action. For example, the heavy bag may be used to help develop power in your side kick, whereas the focus glove can be used to help develop your speed and accuracy of the same kick against a moving target. The inclusion of equipment training is vital if you don't happen to have a live training partner to work out with.

The 'Art' of Training with Equipment

Training can at times become tedious for any martial artist, no matter how dedicated or enthusiastic they might be. However, by training with a variety of equipment you can not only stimulate your interest and challenge your coordination, but when combined with proper use of imagination, can help you avoid boredom and stagnation in your training. The primary goal when training with martial art training equipment is to create or duplicate actual fighting conditions you may encounter as closely as possible. One of the most important things to remember about using any form of training equipment is that the equipment is only as good as the person using it, or the ability of the trainer or coach to use it to its greatest advantage when holding it. The person who holds the training equipment during a training session is commonly referred to as the "feeder" because they set the equipment in various positions and literally "feed" you targets and lines of attack. The ability to feed training equipment well is an art unto itself. It requires not only a comprehensive understanding of combative motions, but also a good imagination in order to achieve the highest levels of training. The trainer decides, dependent upon their skill, on the quality of workout their training partner will receive. The trainer can be cooperative or uncooperative. They can change rhythm suddenly and without warning or provoke a response by attacking the student. A trainer who is very skilled at feeding equipment can get you "emotionally involved" in the work being done, and leave you feeling exhausted yet exhilarated at the end. For any martial art instructor, the correct holding and feeding of martial arts equipment can be a one of the major determining factor in a student's growth.

When you are training by yourself and using any form of fixed equipment such as the heavy bag or the top-and-bottom bag, the use of one's imagination is crucial. It's important that you don't view the equipment as just a non-living, motionless blob that you simply bang away on, but rather, imagine it to be a real opponent that is moving and fighting, and maintain your "combative awareness" at all times while training on it. Regardless of whether you're training on fixed equipment or equipment being held by a training partner, remember that your physical actions are only fifty percent of the equation. The other half of your workout is mental, so you should train your body and mind at the same time. Invest each of your workouts and every one of your actions with "emotional content", by which I mean physical and mental intensity and energy. Keep your training "alive" by using your imagination to the fullest and avoiding any sort of "robotic", non-thinking repetition. Be original and creative in your training, but don't get so caught up in developing countless different drills that you lose sight of the ultimate objective.

Finally, recognize that any form of training equipment has limitations, and that overuse of any particular piece of equipment may negatively affect the transfer of skill. For example, if you spend too much time working out on the heavy bag without doing any form of speed work, you may end up actually slowing the speed of your movements or developing "over-preparation" before your actions, which will telegraph your intentions.

How this book is designed

Any martial artist seriously interested in his or her own personal growth will gain from the material within this book. It is concerned with the cultivation of <u>you</u> as a martial artist, regardless of the style or methods you train in, and offers comprehensive and cohesive training information that will help you improve as a martial artist. How you use this book is entirely up to you. Make it relate to yourself and your own training needs, goals and desires. You can go through it from beginning to end, or you can take one section as you need or want it. Each chapter is devoted to a particular piece of equipment and includes not only examples of various types of actions that can be practiced on the equipment, but also examples of such things as the correct and incorrect way to hold the equipment, safety in training, etc. There are chapters devoted to what I refer to as "mobile" equipment such as focus mitts, kicking shields, etc., which is equipment that is portable and can easily be carried in a training bag or your car, allowing you to work out in different locations both indoors and outdoors. Other chapters are devoted to what I refer to as "fixed" equipment such as the heavy bag, wooden dummy, etc. This is equipment that remains in one location, be it a martial art school, your garage, or wherever.

Keep in mind that while this book illustrates certain techniques or actions both singly and in combination, that is not what it's about. Use the material within this book in conjunction with other training materials such as videotapes, DVDs, etc., to improve your understanding of, and performance in martial art. I delight in constantly searching for new and innovative ways to utilize a piece of training equipment and enjoy it when someone shows me how they've developed or adapted something for their own use. That's what it's all about, developing free-thinking, creative martial artists.

Finally, remember that equipment training should be looked at as a means to an end and not the end in itself. Use your common sense and don't spend valuable time and energy coming up with overly elaborate or esoteric exercises or drills. Keep it simple and functional. Right, let's get down to work!

NOTE: For the sake of clarity, in some of the photos or sequences of photos the feeder's arms may be deliberately held down or open in order for the reader to more clearly see the actions on the equipment. It is not an endorsement of sloppiness with regard to either the person feeding of equipment or the person training on it.

CHAPTER ONE

Focus Gloves

The focus gloves, or focus mitts/pads as they're also called, are without doubt one of the most versatile and useful pieces of training equipment that any martial artist can use to develop, hone and maintain their fighting skills. There are numerous types of focus gloves available on the market today. Some have a larger striking surface and are thicker to help cushion heavier blows. Others are smaller and are designed to help you increase your precision and accuracy and striking. Some are straight and some are slightly curved to fit the hand. Some of the newest versions are even shaped like a human head. Which type you like is a matter of personal preference.

Used correctly either singly or in a pair, focus gloves allow you to utilize all of your offensive and defensive skills in every conceivable way, and are an invaluable tool for helping you:

- Develop proper and efficient body-mechanics in all different types of blows such as kicks, punches, slaps, elbows, or knees.
- Develop your evasive body motions such as slipping, snapping away, bobbing and weaving, and ducking.
- Build precision and accuracy in striking.
- Develop proper timing and distance for speed and power.
- Train "non-telegraphic" movement in your actions.
- Develop good defensive coverage and quick recovery skills.
- Develop the ability to shift from one method or form of attack to another.

As their name suggests, the focus gloves are used primarily to help train you how to 'focus' the energy or power behind your blows. My teacher, Dan Inosanto related to me how he once held the gloves for two hours for Bruce Lee while the latter worked on developing the body-mechanics of a particular kick until he had it just the way he wanted it. The person holding the gloves can control height and distance at which they are set, they can strike at you before or after you have worked an action, or they can alter the distance by opening it or closing it. In the hands of a competent trainer who knows how to feed them properly, focus gloves can literally take you as close to sparring as possible without actually putting the gloves on and "going for it".

Holding of the Focus Gloves Properly

While there might be minor variations amongst trainers with regard to how to hold or feed the focus gloves, knowing how to hold them correctly is an important aspect of training safely with them. Holding them incorrectly may lead to possible injury to the feeder, especially if the person hitting the gloves is very powerful, or accidentally hits the glove when you're not prepared. On the other hand, if the feeder holds the glove at the wrong angle, the person striking the gloves may injure their hand, foot, etc. The following are examples of some common mistakes made by people when they hold the focus gloves, accompanied by correct feeding methods:

1. ARM HELD TOO FAR BACK – By holding the arm too far back in a stretched position, your arm has little room to move if the glove is hit with a powerful blow, and this can cause excess stress on shoulder joint. In this case, when the partner lands a powerful side kick, the feeder's shoulder joint can be over-extended and injured *(below)*.

CORRECT – By giving the arm room to move when the glove is kicked the feeder removes the risk of having his shoulder hurt *(below)*.

2. ARM LOCKED STRAIGHT – If you keep your arm straight with your elbow in a locked position, you put excess stress on the elbow joint and risk possible hyper-extension of your elbow if your partner lands very forceful or unexpected blow. In this example the partner lands a hook kick when the feeder in unprepared, hyper-extending his elbow joint. *(See photos on next page.)*

CORRECT – By keeping a slight bend in his arms at all times, the feeder avoids or reduces the potential of having his arm hyper-extended *(below)*.

3. HAND BENT TOO FAR BACK – If your hand is bent too far backwards when you are holding the glove it can cause stress on wrist joint when the glove is hit. In this example, the partner lands a heavy rear cross punch to the glove, bending the feeder's hand backward. *(See photos below and on next page.)*

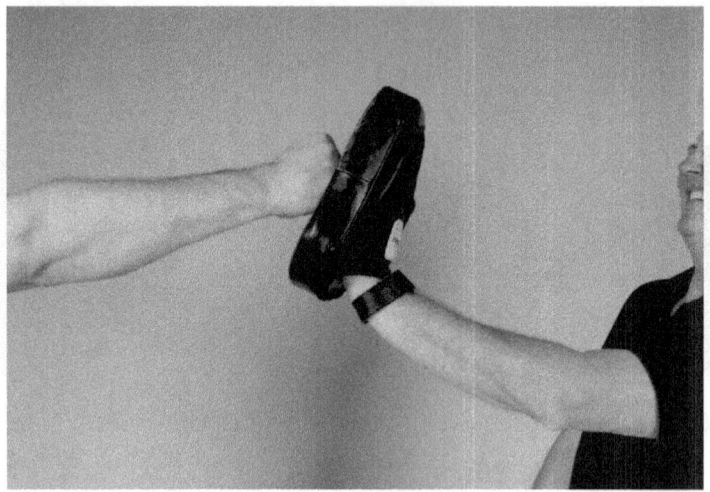

CORRECT – By keeping the wrist properly aligned with the forearm, the feeder prevents his wrist from being bent backward (*Below*).

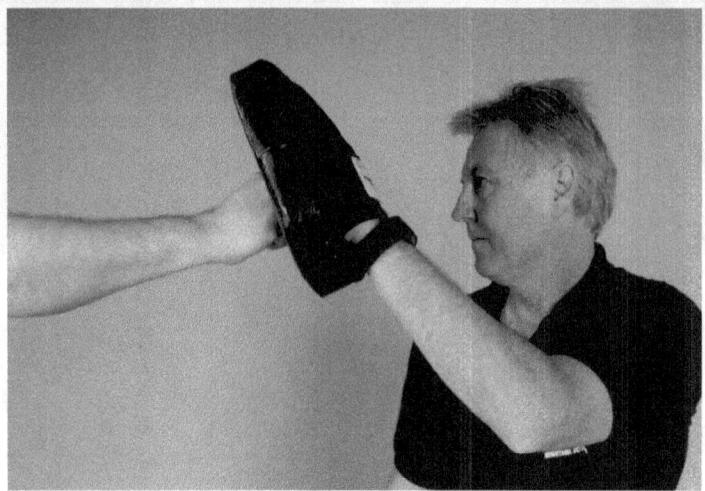

4. ABSORBING FULL FORCE OF BLOW —If you try to hold your arm rigidly where it is instead of dissolving some of the impact by moving slightly with the blow, you absorb the full impact of the strike into your arm. In this example, the feeder holds his arm rigidly in place when his partner lands a powerful hook punch which puts tremendous torque on his elbow joint *(below)*.

CORRECT – By absorbing some of the force of the blow by allowing his arm to move slightly as the blow lands, the feeder prevents his elbow joint from being injured. (NOTE: This does not mean the feeder allows his arm to swing wildly away or moves it before the blow lands *(below)*.

5. PLACING GLOVE AGAINST CERTAIN AREAS OF YOUR BODY – While this method of holding the gloves may be suitable for advanced trainers and practitioners, placing the gloves against areas of your body such as the inside of your thigh or the back of your knee (especially close to joint areas) offers the possibility of serious injury to you should the training partner miss the target. In this example, the partner misses the focus gloves placed against the feeder's thigh and kicks him in the knee joint *(below)*.

CORRECT – By holding the gloves slightly in front of his thigh, the feeder removes the potential of his knee being injured should the kicker miss *(below)*.

6. HOLDING THE GLOVES TOO CLOSE TO YOUR FACE – If you hold the gloves too close to your face and the person hitting the gloves misses the target, they might hit your face. In this example, the feeder holds the glove too close to his face, and when the partner misses the glove with his rear cross, he hits the feeder. *(See photos on next page.)*

CORRECT – By holding the gloves far enough away from your face the poorly aimed punch will not hit you if it misses the target *(below)*.

7. SETTING INCORRECT OR POOR TARGETS – It's important that when feeding the gloves, you set true or realistic targets, as opposed to holding the gloves too wide, too low, etc. In this example, the feeder holds the gloves too far apart, which results in the partner using wide, looping punches instead of crisp economical lines when working a rear cross, lead hook punch combination *(below)*.

CORRECT – By setting compact, realistic the feeder helps his partner develop economical punches *(below)*.

8. MOVING THE GLOVE AS PARTNER HITS – While there is an exercise in which the feeder moves the glove if the person hitting the gloves telegraphs their intentions, it is really an advanced exercise. In normal training you should never pull the glove away as your partner is striking it, as they might hyperextend their arm or leg. In this example, the feeder pulls the glove away as their partner is firing a lead straight punch and the latter hyper-extends his elbow joint.

CORRECT – Keeping the glove where it is until the training partner's blow lands. *(See photos on next page.)*

TRAINING TIP – One thing I've discovered during my years of teaching is that when feeding the focus gloves, the person striking them many times has a tendency to subconsciously adjust their actions to the distance of the person holding the gloves instead of the glove itself, which can cause problems such as the trainer getting hit. The person hitting the gloves has to keep in mind that the gloves represent the targets on the opponent such as the face, leg, etc., and maintain the proper distance. As a feeder you may have to remind your training partner that the gloves are the opponent, not your face or body.

The Various Combative Weapons

The following examples illustrate how to hold the focus gloves for various single offensive actions:

a) Feet
   1) Lead upward snap kick

2) Lead hook kick (3 levels)

- Low

- Medium

- High

3) Lead side kick (3 levels)

- Low

- Medium

- High

4) Lead inverted hook kick (3 levels)

- Low

- Medium

- High

5) Lead sweep kick (3 levels)
- Low

- Medium

- High

6) Rear upward snap kick

7) Rear hook kick (3 levels)
   • Low

   • Medium

- High

8) Rear inward crescent kick

9) Lead outward crescent kick

10) Spinning side/back kick

b) Hands

1) Backfist

2) High lead straight

3) High rear straight/cross

4) Low lead straight

5) Low rear straight/cross

6) High lead hook (fist)

7) High lead hook (palm)

8) High rear hook (fist)

FOCUS GLOVES

9) High rear hook (palm)

10) Low lead hook (fist)

11) Low lead hook (palm)

13) Low rear hook (palm)

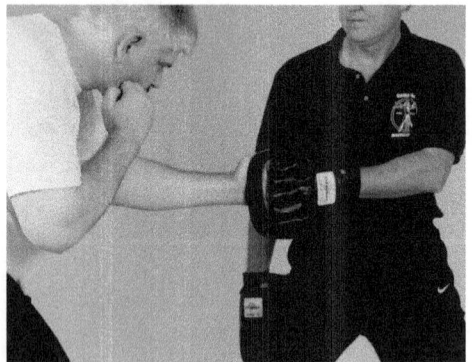

14) Lead uppercut to chin

15) Rear uppercut to chin

16) Lead uppercut to body

17) Rear uppercut to body

18) Rear overhand

19) Lead shovel hook

20) Rear shovel hook

c) Elbows

1) High rear straight

2) High rear diagonal down

3) High lead hook (inwards)

4) High rear hook (inwards)

5) Rear diagonal upward

6) Lead diagonal upward

7) High lead outwards

8) High rear outwards

9) High lead backward

10) High rear backward

11) Lead to body

12) Rear to body

d) Knees

1) Lead vertical knee from medium distance

2) Rear vertical knee from medium distance

3) Lead vertical knee from close-range tie-up position

4) Rear vertical knee from close-range tie-up position

5) Lead diagonal/horizontal inward knee

6) Rear diagonal/horizontal inward knee

e) Other

1) Lead inside forearm smash

2) Rear inside forearm smash

Training the Various Methods of Offensive Actions

When training with focus gloves, you can work simple actions or compound actions. Simple actions consist of any single motion executed in one tempo or beat, such as a lead straight punch, a rear diagonal downward elbow, or a lead side kick. (Examples of simple actions, also known as *Single Direct Attack*, were shown in the previous section). Compound attacks are actions that are comprised of two or more motions and are often referred to as either *Attack by Combination* (such as a lead straight punch to lead hook punch) or *Progressive Indirect Attack.* (such as a low lead hook kick feint to high lead backfist). Also included in this section is the use of what are referred to as *Hand Immobilization Attacks,* in which either one or both of the opponent's upper limbs are immobilized for a split second during the offensive action. The following examples illustrate the various ways or methods of attack and how you can train them on the focus gloves. They are accompanied by the application of the same action in a combative situation.

Attack by Combination (2 movements)

An Attack by Combination is a compound offensive action comprised of two or more movements that flow from one to the next in a well-planned, natural sequence, and are usually thrown to more than one target area (leg-head, head-body, etc.). Feints and false attacks may be included with real attacks in the use of an Attack by Combination.

1) **Foot-Foot** – slide-step low lead hook kick, slide-step lead inverted hook kick.

2) Foot-Foot – slide-step lead side kick to rear spin kick.

38

3) Hand-Hand – low lead straight punch to high lead palm hook.

4) Hand-Hand – high lead straight punch to high rear hook.

5) Foot-Hand – slide-step inverted hook kick to lead straight punch high (R/L).

6) Hand-Foot – High lead backfist to low lead heel hook kick.

7) Hand-Elbow – High lead uppercut to rear diagonal downward elbow.

8) Elbow-Knee – High lead elbow hook to rear vertical upward knee.

9) **Knee-Elbow** – slide-step lead upward knee to rear horizontal elbow.

Attack by Combination (3 movements)

1) **Foot-Foot-Hand** – lead inverted hook kick, lead side kick, lead backfist *(See photos below and on next page.)*

2) Foot-Hand-Foot - lead hook kick, lead backfist, lead side kick.

3) **Hand-Foot-Hand** – high lead backfist to high inverted hook kick to low lead straight punch.

4) **Foot-Hand-Elbow** – low lead front upward snap kick to high palm hook to rear diagonal upward elbow. *(See photos below and on next page.)*

5) **Hand-Elbow-Knee** – rear uppercut to high lead elbow hook to rear vertical upward knee.

Use of Feints/False Attacks in Attack by Combination

When working a particular combination attack such as a lead straight – rear cross – lead uppercut, all three blows do not have to hit. One or more of the blows may be feints or false attacks designed to draw a reaction or open a particular line for the final blow. For example, you might:

1) **Hit-Hit-Hit** – All three punches hit the gloves.

2) **Feint-Hit-Hit** – The first action is a feint, and the final two hits land. *(See photos below and on next page.)*

3) Feint-Feint-Hit – The first two actions are feints or false attacks, and only the final blow lands.

4) Hit-Feint-Hit – In this example, the first punch is real, the second action is a feint, and the third punch is real.

Progressive Indirect Attack

Progressive Indirect Attack involves using an initial feint or false attack to draw some form of defensive reaction such as a block or parry, then deceiving the defensive motion and scoring in the opening line. The two primary differences between this form of attack and Attack By Combination is that in Progressive Indirect Attack (a) the movement flows continually forward, hence the term "progressive", and (b) only the final blow or blows are intended to score. The following are examples of training Progressive Indirect Attack with the focus gloves:

1) Foot-Foot – close the distance with a slide-step lead upward snap kick feint, shifting into a high lead hook kick.

2) Foot-Hand – Close the distance with a slide-step low lead hook kick feint, shifting into a high lead backfist.

3) Hand-Hand – Feint a low rear cross to the opponent's stomach while closing the distance, shifting into a high lead hook.

5) Hand-Elbow – Feint a lead shovel hook while closing the distance, shifting into a rear diagonal downward elbow.

5) Knee-Hand – Close the distance with a slide-step lead upward knee feint, shifting into a lead straight punch.

Attack by Drawing

Attack by Drawing is essentially a form of counter-fighting that consists of provoking an offensive or counter-offensive reaction from an opponent by, which you then use to complete your own attack. In other words, you "lure" or "bait" the opponent with an apparent opening or executing an action that they may attempt to counter, and then counterattack them as they take the bait. Attack by Drawing is a little bit more difficult to train on the focus gloves but can and should be done. The following examples illustrate training Attack by Drawing on the gloves:

1) Use a step-slide retreat to draw the trainer to step forward, and score with a lead hand straight punch as he steps.

2) Use a step-slide advance to draw the trainer's lead hook, counter with a rear overhand left. *(See photos below and on next page.)*

3) Use an open low lead feint to draw the trainer's attempted rear cross stop-hit, which you counter with a lead hook over his arm.

Hand Immobilization Attack

Hand Immobilization Attack, which is also referred to as *trapping hands,* is an offensive action which momentarily immobilizes one or both of the opponent's arms to either score a hit, or draw a reaction which can be used against the opponent. This type of offensive action can be useful not only for striking an opponent, but also to tie up an opponent's arms and offset their abilities to strike you as you close the distance against them. Hand Immobilization Attacks can also when fighting at closer range and to help set up grappling actions. The following examples illustrate how single Hand Immobilization Attacks can be trained with the focus gloves:

1) **Pak sao (high outside)** – From a high outside reference position, use a left hand pak sao (slapping hand) to immobilize the opponent's lead arm as you score with a lead straight punch.

2) **Pak sao (high inside)** – From a high inside reference position, use a left hand pak sao to immobilize the opponent's lead arm as you simultaneously disengage and hit with a lead backfist.

3) **Pak sao (low outside)** – From a low outside reference position, immobilize the opponent's lead arm with a low pak sao as you hit with a high backfist.

3) Lop sao (high outside) – From a high outside reference position, immobilize the opponent's lead arm with a lead hand lop sao (grabbing/pulling arm) while simultaneously hitting with your rear straight punch.

Bridging from Kicking to Trapping

You should be able to bridge from kicking range into Hand Immobilization Attack. In this example, you bridge the gap using a low lead shin/knee hook kick, then fire a low lead hand to the opponent's stomach, and as the opponent attempts to block downward with his lead arm, you trap his arm and backfist him with your lead hand.

Trapping from Unattached Position

Some trapping actions can be used from an unattached position. For example, if the opponent keeps their lead arm too extended, you can trap it with a pak sao as you hit with a backfist.

Trapping Off the Opponent's Attack

You can also practice trapping off of the opponent's offensive action. For example, if the opponent uses attacks with a slow lead jab, you can use pak sao to intercept and shut his attack down as you simultaneously launch your own attack.

HIA Combinations

The following examples illustrate how you can work various hand immobilization combinations on the focus gloves:

1) Attack with a low lead straight punch, and if the opponent uses a lead hand downward block, trap his blocking arm while simultaneously hitting with a lead backfist his face. When the opponent attempts to use a rear hand cross block, use your left hand to trap the arm and hit with another backfist.

2) Attack with a low lead straight punch, and when the opponent uses a rear hand downward block, use a disengagement to evade the block and hit with a high palm hook while simultaneously trapping the opponent's lead arm. If the opponent attempts to block your palm hook with his left hand, use both hands to jerk the opponent's arms down and open the line, then trap them and hit with a lead straight punch.

3) Attack with a high lead backfist, and as the opponent attempts to block it with his lead arm, use a lead hand pulling trap combined with a rear straight punch. As the opponent attempts to use a rear hand outward parry against the strike, trap the arm with another pulling hand trap as you hit with a lead straight punch.

Shifting from HIA Into Other Forms of Attack

The following examples illustrate training the ability to shift from trapping into other forms of attack:

1) **Trapping to Kicking:** as you attempt to trap the opponent's lead arm with pak sao they manage to escape and retreat to long range -- immediately close the distance with a side kick.

2) Trapping to Punching: As you trap the opponent's lead arm with a low pak sao and high backfist, the opponent attempts to slip outside the punch -- immediately fire a rear uppercut followed by a lead hook.

3) Trapping to Elbowing: Use a lead hand lop sao and rear straight punch to pull the opponent into a lead elbow to the ribs.

4) Trapping to Kneeing: Use a high inside to outside jao sao (running hand) to move to a double outside hand position, followed by a two-handed jut sao (jerking hand) with lead vertical knee.

Shifting Between the Various Ways of Attack

A primary goal in martial art training is to develop the fluidity of being able to shift or switch from one method or type of attack (kicking to punching, punching to trapping, etc.) into another without having to even think about it. The moment an opportunity or target presents itself the attack is already on the way.

IMPORTANT POINT – Jeet Kune Do, as Bruce Lee originally developed it, is a principle-centered martial art training process which does away with "compartmentalizing" combative elements into separate elements with different names such as Western Boxing punching, Wing Chun Gung Fu trapping, Thai Boxing elbowing, etc., and instead simply looks at things in terms of 'motion'. A punch is, as they say, simply a punch; a kick is simply a kick. However, for the ease of the reader I've used certain terms in this section of the book. The following examples illustrate shifting from one method or form of attack to another:

Shifting from Straight Blast into Western Boxing Punching

In the midst of using a straight blast, the trainer shifts the targets into western boxing, in this example, a rear uppercut, lead hook, rear cross combination.

In the midst of using a straight blast, the trainer takes a small step backward and shifts the targets, in this case into a lead hook to the body, followed by a lead hook to the face and rear uppercut to the solar plexus.

Shifting from Straight Blast into Elbowing

In the midst of using a straight blast, the trainer shifts the targets and you immediately flow into a lead elbow hook followed by a rear horizontal elbow. *(See photos below and on next page.)*

Shifting from Straight Blast into Elbowing

In the midst of using a straight blast, the trainer suddenly shifts the targets and you immediately flow into a rear diagonal upward elbow, followed by a lead elbow hook and rear diagonal downward elbow.

Shifting from Straight Blast into Kicking

In the midst of using a straight blast, the trainer slides-steps out to long distance and sets the midsection-level lead hook kick line.

In the midst of your using a straight blast, the trainer slide-steps back and sets the low side kick line. *(See photos on next page.)*

Shifting from Straight Blast into Kneeing

In the midst of using a straight blast, the trainer suddenly sets the focus gloves at groin level, and you immediately fire a slide-step lead upward vertical knee. *(See photos below and on next page.)*

Shifting from Straight Blast into Kneeing

In the midst of using a straight blast, the trainer shifts the target to groin level and you grab him around his neck and fire a rear upward vertical knee.

Shifting from Straight Blast into Trapping (HIA)

In the midst of using a straight blast, the trainer blocks your right hand inward with his lead arm, immediately trap his arm with a left hand pak sao as you simultaneously disengage and hit with your lead backfist.

Shifting from Straight Blast into Trapping (HIA)

In the midst of using a straight blast, as the trainer uses a rear hand inward block against your right arm, immediately allow the force to continue through by using the "hinge principle" as you use a left hand lop sao to grab his left arm and backfist the right glove.

Now let's examine some methods of shifting into the straight blast from other forms of attack:

Shifting from Kicking into Straight Blast

Bridge the gap from long-range with a low lead side kick, and immediately flow into the straight blast.

Close from long-range with a lead hook kick/rear hook kick combination (trainer uses drop-step back to switch leads), plant left leg forward into left lead and launch your straight blast.

Shifting from Western Boxing into Straight Blast

Trainer sets a high lead straight, low rear cross, high lead hook combination, then shifts targets to indicate the straight blast.

Shifting from Elbowing into Straight Blast

From close-range, work a high lead elbow hook, rear diagonal down elbow combination, and immediately flow into the straight blast.

Shifting from Trapping (HIA) into Straight Blast

Close the distance with a low lead straight punch, and as opponent attempts to block the punch downward with his lead arm, trap his arm with a low pak sao while hitting with a high backfist, then move into your straight blast. *(See photos below and on next page.)*

Shifting from Kneeing to the Straight Blast

From a grappling tie up position around the trainer's neck, fire a lead knee followed by a rear knee, then shove the trainer backward and straight blast as he sets the line.

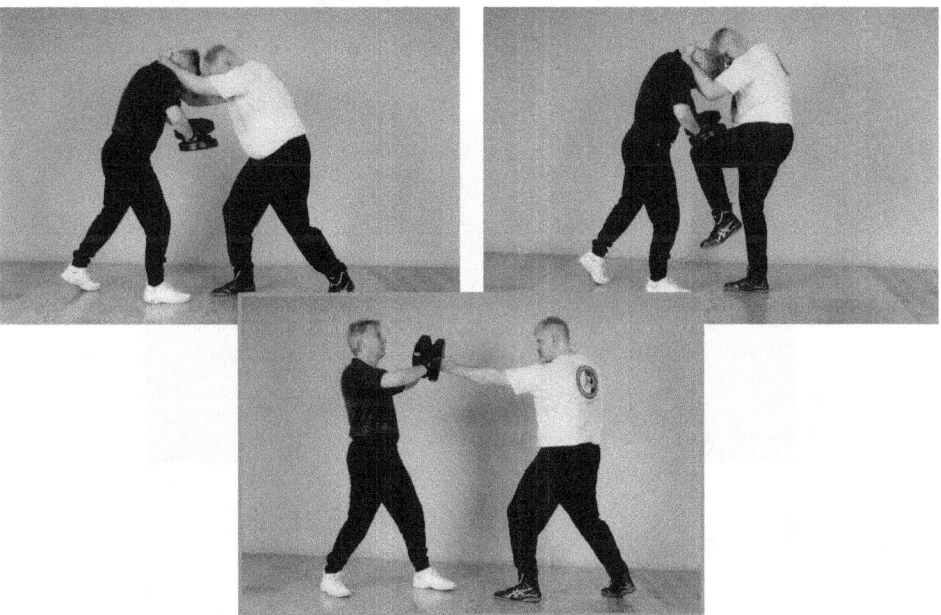

Working Various Distances

Another important factor in training with focus gloves is working all of the various ranges or distances (long, medium, close), and developing your ability to immediately relate and adjust to the distance as it changes or shifts. The following examples illustrate how to shift from one distance to another:

CLOSING FROM LONG DISTANCE TO MEDIUM RANGE – (shifting from kicking to hitting, etc.)

a) Close from long-range with a lead side kick into high lead backfist, high rear cross.

b) Close from long-range with low lead hook kick into low lead straight punch to high lead backfist.

CLOSING FROM LONG DISTANCE INTO CLOSE RANGE – (shifting from kicking to close-range punching, or elbowing, kneeing, etc.)

a) Close from long-range with a low lead front kick followed by a high lead straight punch, high lead hook, to rear diagonal downward elbow.

b) Close with low lead side kick, followed by a high lead backfist into rear upward knee.

SHIFTING FROM CLOSE RANGE TO MEDIUM DISTANCE – (relating to opening distance by shifting from hitting, elbowing to medium range punching, kicking etc.)

    a) Shift from lead diagonal upward elbow to high rear cross and stationary low lead hook kick.

b) Shift from tie-up position with lead upward knee to rear horizontal elbow, lead palm hook high to stationary rear hook kick.

JEET KUNE DO

SHIFTING FROM CLOSE RANGE TO LONG DISTANCE – (relate to the opening distance by shifting from close range attacks (punching, elbowing) to long range kicking).

a) Lead hook high to rear uppercut high to slide-step lead hook kick as trainer moves back to long-range.

b) Lead elbow hook high, into high lead backfist followed by rear spin kick.

Maintaining Correct Distance While Feeding Lines

It's very important that, when working on compound attacks involving a shift or change in the weapons being used (such as shifting from punching to kicking), that the trainer sets the correct distance for the various actions. If the trainer sets the target either too close or too far, the student may develop between an incorrect sense of distance and either the trainer or the student may end up getting injured. The following examples illustrate correct and incorrect distance setting:

CORRECT DISTANCE — Following a lead straight, rear cross, the trainer uses a slide-step retreat to move out to long range and set the hook kick target.

INCORRECT DISTANCE (TOO CLOSE) — Although the trainer retreats to long range, he holds the target too far forward, and as a result gets kicked in the arm. *(See photos below and on next page.)*

INCORRECT DISTANCE (TOO FAR) — This time the trainer retreats too far and causes his partner to miss the glove completely.

Proper Depth of Penetration in Striking

The correct depth of penetration of any strike is an integral facet of developing the highest degree of power and "explosiveness" in a blow. If, for instance, you penetrate too deeply with your strike, the blow may be smothered and turn into more of a 'push' or 'shove'. On the other hand, if you don't penetrate deep enough, the blow will become too much of a 'flick' and have little or no effect upon the opponent. Some people will get very technical and say things like "Your punch should penetrate 2 inches." That's all fine and well if you are hitting a stationary target. But in an actual combative situation the target is likely to not only be moving, but also trying to hit you. The basic principle to remember for proper penetration is to aim the attack several inches through where the target is going to be when the blow lands. (For a training method you can use to develop explosiveness in kicking, punching, or any type of blow, refer to the "water principle" and "whip principle" training exercise which is detailed in my book, *The Encyclopedia of JKD*.)

a) **INCORRECT PENETRATION (TOO CLOSE)** – By penetrating too deeply with a lead straight punch, the blow becomes more of a "push."

b) **INCORRECT PENETRATION (TOO FAR)** – At the other extreme, by not penetrating sufficiently, the blow becomes a non-powerful "flick."

c) CORRECT DEPTH OF PENETRATION – By aiming the punch several inches past the glove, the blow develops maximum power.

TRAINING DEFENSIVE SKILLS

While the previous section dealt with training offensive skills, you can and should develop all of your defensive skills with the aid of the focus gloves. For simplicity and clarity, the various single and compound defensive actions that can be developed with the gloves are being illustrated without counters or follow-ups.

Single Defensive Actions

a) **Push-shuffle retreat** – use a quick push shuffle retreat to evade a lead straight punch to the face.

b) Snap Away – use an upper body snap away to evade a rear cross to the face.

c) Slip inside and out – use an outside slip to evade a lead straight punch to the face.

d) **Slip inside and out** – use an outside slip to evade a rear straight punch to the face.

e) **Duck under** – use a duck under to evade a rear hook punch to the face.

f) **Bob and weave** – use a bob and weave to evade a rear hook punch to the face.

g) Shoulder roll away (against high/low punches) – use a shoulder roll to evade a rear cross to the face.

h) Covering – use a rear arm cover to protect against a lead hook punch to the head.

i) Covering – use a lead arm cover to protect against a rear hook punch to the head.

j) Covering – use a rear arm cover to protect against a lead hook punch to the body.

k) Covering – use a lead arm cover to protect against a rear hook punch to the body.

l) Forearm deflection – use a rear forearm to deflect a lead straight punch to the body.

m) Forearm deflection – use a lead forearm to deflect a lead straight punch to the body.

n) Scoop Parry – use a lead hand scoop parry against a low straight punch to the body.

o) Scoop Parry – use a rear hand scoop parry against a low straight punch to the body.

p) Shoulder stopping – use a lead-hand shoulder stop against a lead hook punch to the head.

q) Shoulder stopping – use a lead-hand shoulder stop against a rear hook punch to the head.

Compound Defensive Actions

1. Snap Away – Bob and Weave: Use an upper body snap away from the trainer's lead jab, then bob and weave under his rear hook to the head. *(See photos below and on next page.)*

2. Snap Away – Bob and Weave: use an upper body snap away from the trainer's rear cross, bob and weave under his lead hook to the head.

3. Bob and Weave – Shoulder Roll: bob and weave under the trainer's lead hook to the head, then shoulder roll away from his high rear cross.

4. Cover – Duck: use a rear forearm cover against the trainer's lead body hook, then duck under his high rear hook.

5. **Shoulder stop – Forearm deflection:** use a lead hand shoulder stop against the trainer's right lead hook, then forearm deflect his right rear uppercut to the body.

6. **Forearm deflect – Scoop parry:** use a lead forearm deflection against the trainer's left rear uppercut, then a lead scooping parry against his right lead uppercut.

Combining Offensive and Defensive Skills:

Fighting is a constantly changing game and often requires the ability to rapidly shift from offense to defense and vice versa. The following examples illustrate how you can combine offensive and defensive skills with the gloves:

1) Hit with your lead straight punch, snap away from trainer's lead straight punch return. *(See photos below and on next page.)*

2) Hit with your lead straight punch, slip outside the trainer's high rear straight return.

3) Hit with your high lead hook, immediately bob and weave under the trainer's high rear hook. *(See photos below and on next page.)*

4) Hit with high rear straight punch, bob and weave under the trainer's high lead hook.

5) Hit with your lead straight punch, rear cover against the trainer's high hook.

6) Close with low lead hook kick to high lead straight punch, bob and weave under the trainer's high lead hook.

Developing Counterattack Skills

A counterattack is an attack made against an opponent's offensive movement, either as they attack on their own initiative or are somehow provoked into attacking. Counter-attack skills include:

- Interception (stop-hit/time-hit)
- Parry and counter
- Evade and counter
- Cover/block and counter

(For a detailed breakdown of each of the various forms of counter-attack, see *The Encyclopedia of JKD*.) The following examples illustrate the various counterattack skills that may be developed with the focus gloves:

a) Interception

1) Intercept the trainer's preparatory forward step with a lead side kick.

2) Intercept the trainer's high rear cross with a low lead hook kick.

3) Intercept the trainer's rear uppercut with a high lead hook.

4) Intercept the trainer's forward step with a high lead straight punch.

5) Intercept the trainer's lead hook to the head with a rear corkscrew hook.

6) Intercept the trainer's lead hook with a lead straight punch (R/L).

7) Intercept the trainer's lead straight punch with a sliding leverage hit (R/L).

b) Parry and Counter

Parry and counter can be performed two ways. One way is that the parry is performed first, followed by the counter. The second way is that the parry and counter are performed simultaneously.

1) Use a rear hand cross parry against the trainer's lead jab, then fire a lead straight punch/rear cross counter.

2) Use a lead hand cross parry against the trainer's lead jab as you fire a low rear cross to lead shovel hook combination. *(See photos on next page.)*

3) Use a scoop parry against the trainer's low lead punch, then fire a high lead backfist to rear uppercut.

4) Use a low slap parry against the trainer's mid-level side kick as you slide-step retreat, straight blast as the opponent recovers forward.

5) Use a rear hand scoop parry combined with a curving right step against the trainer's mid-level lead hook kick, return lead straight, rear cross, lead body hook punching combination.

c) Evade and Counter

As with parry and counter, evade and counter can be used two ways. One way is to evade the attack first and then counter. The second is to evade and counter the attack at the same time. The following examples illustrate training evade and counter:

1) Evade the trainer's low rear hook kick by using a step through retreat, then immediately counter with a low right front kick feint into a high hook kick.

2) Use a push shuffle retreat to evade the trainer's lead hook to the head, immediately push shuffle back in and counter with the straight blast.

3) Sidestep outside the trainer's high lead jab, then counter with a high rear cross.

4) Slip outside the trainer's high rear cross, then counter with a lead shovel hook.

5) Roll away from the trainer's high rear cross as you simultaneously counter with a high lead hook.

6) Bob and weave under the trainer's high lead hook and counter with a lead elbow hook to the body, followed by a high rear diagonal downward elbow from the outside position.

7) Slip outside the trainer's high lead jab and simultaneously counter with lead straight punch to the ribs.

8) Duck underneath the trainer's high rear cross and counter with low rear cross to the stomach.

9) Lift lead leg to evade the trainer's rear oblique kick, counter with a high lead straight, high lead hook punching combination.

d) Cover/Block and Counter

Blocking is usually considered the least efficient of all defensive skills because it usually involves force against force, which may not be in your best interest, especially if the opponent is bigger, stronger and more powerful than you. However, for one reason or another, covering and blocking may become the only course of action left open to you, so you should learn how to dissipate or absorb an opponent's force as safely as possible. The following examples illustrate the use of cover/block and counter in training:

1) Use a rear forearm cover against a high hook to the head, counter with a lead shovel hook to the body followed by a lead hook to the head.

2) Use a rear forearm cover against a high long palm hook (to simulate a kick) to the ribs, counter with the straight blast.

3) Use a lead forearm cover against a low rear cross, return high rear cross, lead body hook followed by a lead elbow hook to the head.
(See photos below and on next page.)

4) Use a rear forearm cover against a lead uppercut to the body, counter with a high lead elbow hook followed by a rear horizontal elbow.

5) Use a shoulder stop against a high lead hook, counter with a rear horizontal elbow followed by a rear vertical knee.

6) Lift lead leg to block a rear hook kick with your shin, counter with a lead straight, rear cross combination.

Other Various Training Methods Using the Focus Gloves

There are numerous other ways of utilizing the focus gloves in training in addition to teaching various strikes or offensive, counter-offensive and defensive skills. Specialized training methods may be used to increase a student's perceptual speed and reaction time, to develop precision and accuracy, improve movement speed, as well as keeping the student aware and alert to attacks either before after they hit the gloves. In certain drills the feeder remains stationary, and in others they may be stationary or moving. The following are examples of some of the various methods of using the focus gloves in training:

GLOVE "FREEZING" DRILL -- The feeder moves the focus glove around and then without warning suddenly stops it. The student's goal is to hit the glove in whatever position it happens to be the moment it stops. This forces the training partner to stay focused and aware. In this example, the partner hits the glove with a straight lead punch the moment the trainer stops moving it.

"FLASH CARDS" DRILL – The feeder uses the focus gloves like "flash cards" to help student develop the perceptual speed in identifying various targets and the corresponding blows that may be used. The primary goal is to cut down the time it takes for the training partner to recognize the lines and respond correctly. In this example the partner hits with a lead uppercut, rear uppercut combination the moment the trainer flashes the lines. *(See photos on next page.)*

HIT AS FEEDER ADVANCES – The student hits a target the moment the trainer moves forward with some type of footwork such as a step-slide advance, thereby catching the opponent moving in. In this example the partner hits with a rear straight punch as the feeder steps forward.

HIT AS FEEDER RETREATS – The student hits the target the moment the trainer moves backward with some form of footwork. This helps teach how to penetrate with your attack. In this example the partner bridges in with a lead straight punch as the feeder steps backward.

HIT AS FEEDER SIDESTEPS -- The student hits an assigned target the moment the trainer moves laterally. In this example the partner fires a lead backfist as the feeder steps to the left.

VISUAL CUE #1 – The student hits the target as quickly as possible as the trainer lowers one arm. (As the student progresses, the trainer can increase the speed with which he moves his arm). In this example the partner fires a rear straight punch as the feeder lowers his lead arm.

VISUAL CUE #2 – The student hits the target the moment the trainer lifts his lead or rear leg. In this example the partner hits with a rear straight punch as the trainer lifts his lead leg.

(See photos on next page.)

JEET KUNE DO

VISUAL CUE #3 – The student hits the target the moment the trainer switches his lead. In this example the partner fires a low rear hook kick as the feeder switches from a right lead to left lead.

"NON-TELEGRAPHIC" DRILL (ADVANCED LEVEL) – In this exercise the trainer pulls the focus glove away before the punch or kick lands if the student telegraphs his strike in any way, such as pulling his arm back before hitting. In this exercise, the person punching should not start from a static or "set" position, but from a state of "small" motion.

CAUTION: This drill should primarily be used for striking with arms as the distance is too great when using legs. But be very careful when using this training method to avoid hyper-extending your arm.
(See photos below and on next page.)

FOCUS GLOVES

"WOBBLY GLOVE" DRILL – In this exercise designed to develop focus of energy in a blow, the feeder lets the glove "wobble" if student doesn't hit the target squarely. In this example, the student doesn't hit the target in the center and the feeder lets the glove wobble.

"HIT AND SET" DRILL – In this exercise the feeder hits student's arms with the focus gloves to simulate an attack, then sets various target lines. This helps train the student to maintain a good on-guard position and be ready to counterattack at all times. In this example, the feeder hits his partner's forearm to simulate a low body blow, then sets a high straight punch line for his partner to strike. *(See photos below and on next page.)*

"SET AND THEN HIT DRILL" – In this exercise the feeder sets the target lines, then attacks student upon completion of his technique. This helps train the student to immediately recover to his on-guard position and be ready to defend himself after completing any action. In this example, the student hits with a high rear straight punch, then uses a forearm cover when the trainer fires a body hook with the other glove.

"CLOSED EYES" DRILL – This drill helps the student increase their speed at recognizing various lines of attack. In the exercise, the trainer sets a particular line or lines while the student has his eyes closed. On a pre-arranged signal, the student opens eyes, recognizes the target line(s) and strikes as quickly as possible. In this example the student snaps his eyes open, recognizes the line and responds with a lead straight punch. *(See photos on next page.)*

FOCUS GLOVES

TACTILE AWARENESS DRILL — These drills can be used to heighten your tactile response during close quarter actions, such as in the midst of using hand immobilization attack or in a tie-up clinch position. In this example, the trainer touches the inside of the student's forearms with the gloves. The instant the trainer pulls one of the gloves away, the student fires an uppercut with the same hand.

TRAINING TIP -- It's important when utilizing any of the above training drills for both the trainer and the person hitting the gloves to maintain the integrity of the exercise and not "cheat" or change it. Doing so will nullify the purpose of the drill and render it less effective or even useless.

Striking to Different Directions

In real life, attacks will not always come from in front of you, but rather from the side or even from behind you. So besides working with the trainer directly in front of you, it's also a good idea to train to be able to strike in different directions with speed, accuracy and power. And you may not have time to move into a fighting stance before firing your weapon, so you should practice firing your combative tools from a relaxed, normal standing position. As with your other forms of training, make sure that whatever actions you train are economical and practical. The following examples illustrate hitting the gloves at different directions from a natural position:

a) Lead side kick to the right

b) Rear hook kick to the left

c) Left back kick to rear

d) Right back kick from lead

e) Right backfist to the right

f) Right high elbow to the rear

g) Right low elbow to the rear

h) Pivot to side off trainer's step-forward visual cue, evade rear hook kick to thigh and counter with side kick.

Working from Ground Positions

Sometimes you may find yourself fighting from the position of being on the ground, or against an opponent on the ground. If you find yourself in such a position it's vital to be able to either use offensive actions or defend yourself and fend off an opponent until you can get back to your feet, as well as fight effectively while on the ground. Various kicks and strikes can be practiced against the focus gloves while (a) you're in a ground fighting position and the opponent is standing, (b) the opponent is on the ground and you are standing, or (c) both you and the opponent are on the ground. Examples of some of these ground actions include:

a) Hook Kick (lead/rear leg)

b) Heel Hook Kick (lead leg)

c) Front Thrusting Kick (lead/rear leg)

d) Side thrust kick (top leg)

e) Side thrust kick (bottom leg)

f) Straight punch (bottom position)

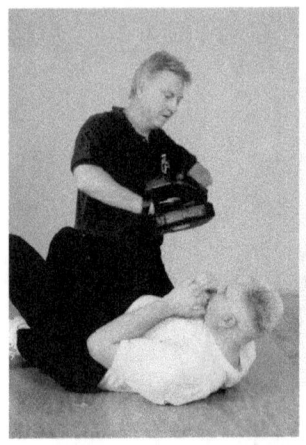 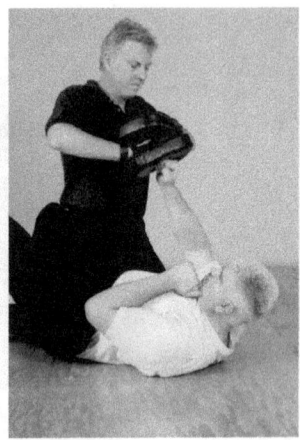 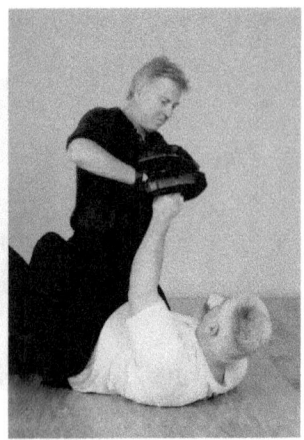

g) Hook punch (bottom position)

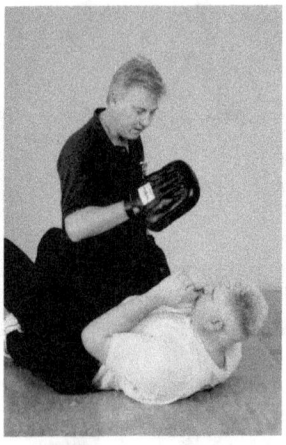 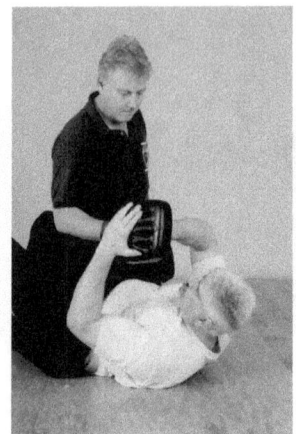

h) Elbow (bottom position)

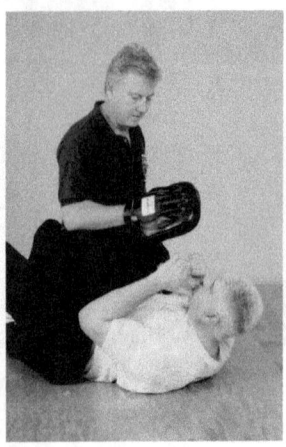 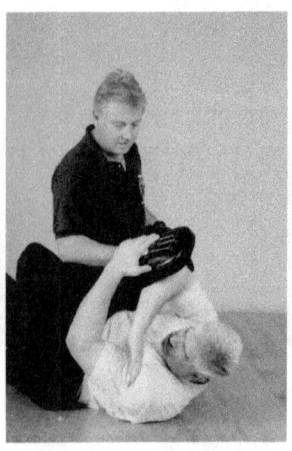

i) Straight punch (top position)

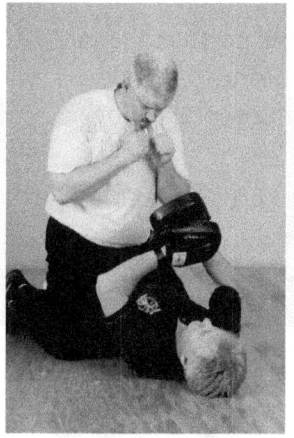 

j) Hook punch (top position)

 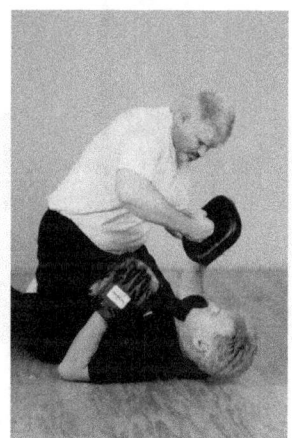

k) Downward elbow (top position)

 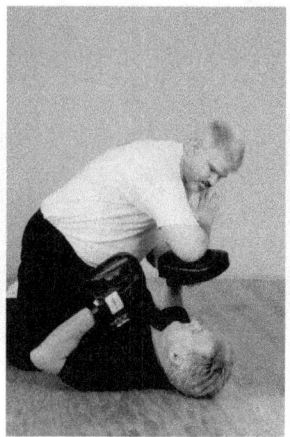

Solo Training with Gloves

If you don't happen to have a training partner available, certain types of strikes may be trained by holding the gloves yourself. The following are examples of solo training on the gloves:

a) Kicking -- Rear inward crescent kick

b) Elbowing – Rear diagonal upward elbow

c) Kneeing – rear vertical upward knee

TRAINING TIPS FOR USING FOCUS GLOVES -- When used correctly the focus gloves are one of the most useful pieces of equipment that any martial artist can train with. You're only limited by your own imagination in developing different methods of using them. Just remember that whatever you do, keep the training as realistic as possible. If you're training a partner or student and want them to develop specific combinations or increase the speed of a combination, make sure they know what the combination is in advance so they don't make mistakes or train incorrectly.

CHAPTER TWO

The Kicking Shield

Another versatile piece of training equipment that can and should be utilized in your martial art training regimen is known as the kicking shield (also referred to as the body-shield). There are various different types of shields available on the market today (air-filled, foam-filled, hard, soft, straight, contoured, heavy, light, etc.). Which type you choose to use is really a matter of personal preference and may depend upon such things as your size and abilities. A 10-year-old beginning martial artist would obviously not require the same type of shield as an advanced adult practitioner. I myself like to use several different types, each of which offers a different feel.

The primary purpose of the kicking shield is to help you develop both correct distance and proper penetration in your kicks against a moving (or sometimes stationary) target. Anyone who has seen the movie, "Way of the Dragon" can't help but remember the scene in which Bruce Lee hits an air shield being held by another actor with a side kick that knocks the man off his feet and catapults him airborne backward into a stack of cardboard boxes. I've spent a lot of time with a number of people who trained with Bruce and who have had the dubious honor of being on the receiving end of one of his famous side kicks into the shield. Larry Hartsell was one of the noted few who managed to hold the shield without being knocked across the room, but said he developed severe headaches whenever he held it for Lee. He later discovered that the headaches were to due to the fact that his neck was literally being whip-lashed by the force of Lee's kicks. A noted black belt karate practitioner who had been on the receiving end of Lee's kicking power described it in the following way, *"The power from his striking and kicking techniques are bursting. He demonstrated a side kick on me that moved so fast that it felt as though my eyeballs were still where I was standing when he hit me."*

In addition to helping you develop the proper application of your kicks, the shield can be used to help develop speed and "suddenness" in your movements. When you're training on it, if you telegraph your intention to kick in any way, the person holding the shield can simply move away from your attack and cause it to miss (be careful to avoid hyper-extending your leg), or close the distance and jam it. You can also use the shield to develop or enhance reaction time and increase your awareness. The shield doesn't have to be used solely for kicking, however. It's a multipurpose tool that can be used for training many of your combative striking tools. You can hit it with your hands, feet, knees, elbows, forearms, and even your shoulder. The great thing about the kicking shield is that it can be used like a mobile heavy bag, with the trainer moving around and setting different targets. As with the focus gloves (or any other piece of training equipment for that matter) the person holding the shield plays a vital role in the effectiveness of its use. How well the trainer uses it to feed the various targets or lines of attack can be a determining factor in how good a workout you get. The holder should be as "alive" as possible, and function as a moving target while advancing, retreating, circling left and right and setting various target lines that simulate attack openings.

Holding the Shield

Like any piece of training equipment, it's very important to hold the kicking shield safely and in the proper manner. Holding it incorrectly offers the potential for injury not only to the person hitting the shield, but also the person striking it. Furthermore, feeding poor target lines can cause the person hitting to develop incorrect or poor body-mechanics.

Incorrect Holding Methods

a) Holding shield too far away from body – By holding the shield too far away from your body, your arms alone will take the full force of the blow and can be injured if you receive a very powerful kick. Also, because the shield is less stable, there is a possibility that your partner's blow could slide off the shield and hit your body instead.

b) Leg locked straight – If you keep your leg too straight when holding the shield against it for low-line kicks, there's a possibility that your knee joint may be injured as the result of a very forceful blow.

c) Leg too sideways – If, when holding for low-line kicks you turn your leg too far sideways, your knee joint may be injured as the result of receiving a very forceful blow.

d) Moving away before blow lands – If you move back or pull the shield away before your partner's blow lands, he or she may injure themselves by hyper-extending their knee joint.

e) Moving into blow – By the same token, if you move into your partner's blow, you may cause them to jam their leg or arm and injure themselves.

THE KICKING SHIELD

f) Standing in poor ready position – If you are not braced in a good ready position, you can be knocked down and possibly injured by a very forceful kick.

Correct Holding Method

While it depends upon how the shield is designed, in most cases the safest method of holding it is to slip one of your forearms through the handles or straps, and use your other hand as a brace on top of the shield. Get yourself into a good ready position and hold the shield firmly but not too tightly against your body for support. Exhale strongly when the kick lands, and if necessary, learn to move or ride with the force of a powerful blow as opposed to absorbing it with your body. Above all, stay alert and focused on the person hitting the shield.

Various Methods of Feeding

You can use a variety of training methods when using the kicking shield. Some methods help you develop your visual awareness or reduce your reaction time, while others allow you to concentrate on finding correct distance and depth of penetration in your strikes. Still others force you to deal with attacks coming from various, different directions. The following examples illustrate some of the ways in which the shield can be used:

a) Holder remains stationary

In this case the trainer remains in a stationary position and sets the target (hook kick, side kick, etc.) while the student practices different types of kicking footwork such as step-and-slide, slide-step, or even kicking from a stationary position.

b) Holder moves forward to close distance

In this method, which helps develop your sense of timing, the student kicks in response to the trainer's forward movement (step-slide, step-thru, etc.), with the goal being for his kick to land before the trainer completes his movement.

c) Holder moves backward to open distance

In this method the student responds to the trainer's backward movement (slide-step, drop-back, etc,) to develop proper penetration against an opponent attempting to escape. The goal is to land your kick either before or just as the trainer is finishing his backward movement.

THE KICKING SHIELD

d) Visual cue

In this method the student watches for a specific visual cue such as lifting leg, switching leads, etc., and reacts with a designated kick as quickly as possible when the cue is given. Besides working a particular striking tool, the goal is to increase your visual perception speed.

e) Kicking to various directions

In real life, attacks do not only come from the front, but often from the side or from behind. In this exercise the student practices kicking to targets set at different positions such as to the right or left side, or behind. The kick or strike chosen will relate to the body position of the person hitting and the line set by the trainer.

Working Various Weapons

The following are examples of the various weapons that can be trained against a kicking shield, as well as the correct way to hold the shield for each type of attack:

a) Kicks (single actions)

1) Lead side kick (low)

2) Lead side kick (medium)

THE KICKING SHIELD

3) Lead hook kick

4) Lead front thrust kick (2 levels)

5) Lead inverted hook kick

6) Rear spinning back kick

7) Rear hook kick

8) Rear oblique kick

b) Knees (single actions)

1) Lead vertical knee (medium range without tie-up)

THE KICKING SHIELD

2) Rear vertical knee (medium range without tie-up)

3) Lead vertical knee (close range with tie-up)

4) Rear vertical knee (close range with tie-up)

5) Lead diagonal/horizontal knee (medium range without tie-up)

6) Rear diagonal/horizontal knee (medium range without tie-up)

7) Lead diagonal/horizontal knee (close range with tie-up)

8) Rear diagonal/horizontal knee (close range with tie-up)

c) Punches (single actions)
1) Low lead straight punch

2) Low rear straight punch

3) Low lead body hook

4) Low rear body hook

5) Low lead shovel hook

6) Low rear shovel hook

7) Low lead uppercut

8) Low rear uppercut

d) Elbows (single actions)
1) Low rear elbow

2) Low lead elbow

3) Backward elbow

e) Other (single actions)

1) Lead shoulder butt

2) Rear shoulder butt

3) Backhand forearm smash to body

CAUTION: *I do not recommend holding the shield at face-level for any type of punching or elbowing to the face or head. This is due to the fact that it is difficult to support it properly and you run the risk of having the blow slide off and hit you instead. It is better to use another type of striking pad such as focus gloves, Thai pads or some other form of striking pad.*

Working the Various Ways of Attack

You can work single/simple actions (any individual motion) or compound actions (any action comprised of two or more motions) against the kicking shield. Simple actions include Single Direct Attack and Single Angulated Attack. Compound actions include Attack by Combination and Progressive Indirect Attack. Examples of Single Direct Attack actions were illustrated in the previous section. The following examples illustrate some of the ways you can use the shield to develop your compound striking skills (for a detailed breakdown of Attack By Combination and Progressive Indirect Attack, as well as the use of feints and false attacks, refer to the chapter on Focus Gloves):

Attack by Combination

1. **Lead side kick, rear spin kick** – Slide up with a lead side kick, then plant forward and rear spinning side kick as trainer retreats and keeps the same target line.

2. Lead inverted hook kick, lead side kick – Slide up with a lead inverted hook kick, plant forward and slide up with a lead side kick as trainer retreats and sets the side kick target line.

3. **Rear hook kick, left side kick** – Fire a stationary rear hook kick, plant forward and slide up with a left lead side kick as trainer retreats and sets the side kick target line.

4. **Feint lead hook kick, lead inverted hook kick** – Close the distance with a lead hook kick feint, followed by a slide-step lead inverted hook kick as trainer drops back into opposite lead and sets the inverted hook kick target line.

5. **Rear oblique kick, lead hook kick** -- Feint a rear oblique kick, use a jump step to flow into a lead hook kick as trainer slide step retreats and sets hook kick target line.

6. **Lead hook kick, lead straight punch** -- Close the distance with a slide-step lead hook kick, plant forward and fire low lead punch (feeder remains stationary as they set the punching line).

7. **Lead side kick, feint high lead backfist, low rear cross** – Close distance with slide-step lead side kick, plant forward and feint a high lead backfist, then drop and fire low rear cross (feeder remains stationary as they set punching line).

8. **Low lead straight punch, low rear cross** – Close the distance with your low lead straight punch to the body, followed by a low rear cross (feeder remains stationary).

9. Lead uppercut to rear uppercut – Fire a lead uppercut to the body, followed by a rear uppercut to the body.

10. Feint lead straight punch, rear uppercut -- Feint low lead straight punch, hit with rear uppercut to the body.

11. **Low rear cross, lead hook kick** – Hit with a low rear cross to the body, followed by a lead hook kick as the trainer retreats and sets the target (feeder opens the distance after low rear cross hits target).

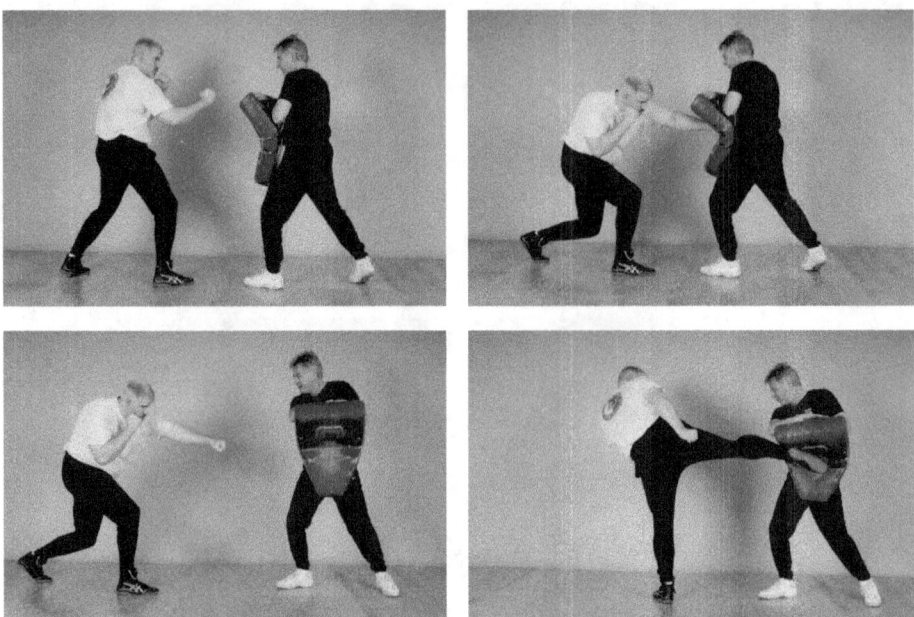

12. **Lead shovel hook, rear hook kick** – Hit with a lead shovel hook to the body, followed by a rear hook kick as the trainer retreats and sets the target (feeder opens the distance after lead shovel hook hits target).

13. **Feint lead finger jab, rear oblique kick** – Feint a lead finger jab to distract the opponent as you hit with a rear oblique kick to the shin or knee (feeder remains stationary).

14. **Lead shovel hook, rear horizontal elbow** – Fire a lead shovel hook to the body, then drop and hit with a rear horizontal elbow to the ribs (feeder remains stationary but pivots body slightly to set elbow target line).

15. Low rear cross, low lead elbow hook – Fire a low rear cross to the body followed by a low lead elbow hook. (feeder remains stationary but pivots body slightly to set elbow target line).

16. Lead uppercut, rear uppercut, grab neck and rear vertical knee – At close range, fire a lead uppercut followed by a rear uppercut, then hook the trainer's neck and fire a rear vertical knee to the body (feeder remains stationary as he sets knee target line).

17. Feint high lead backfist, lead vertical knee – Feint a high lead backfist to distract the opponent as you slide up with a lead vertical upward knee (feeder remains stationary).

18. Feint rear diagonal downward elbow, hook neck and rear vertical knee – At close range, feint a rear diagonal downward elbow, then hook the opponent's neck and fire a rear vertical upward knee to the body or face (feeder remains stationary).

19. Feint high lead jab, shoulder butt – Feint a high lead jab, then shoot in and shoulder butt to the ribs (feeder remains stationary).

Progressive Indirect Attack

1) Feint low lead front kick to close distance and draw reaction, shift to mid-level lead hook kick.

2) Feint mid-level inverted hook kick to draw reaction, shift to low stomping side kick.

3) Feint high lead hook to close distance and draw reaction, shift to low rear cross.

4) Feint high lead hook punch to close distance and draw reaction, shift to rear diagonal downward elbow.

Combining Footwork with Kicking

Another important factor for any martial artist is the ability to combine their attacking and counterattacking actions with different types of footwork. The following examples illustrate some of the ways in which kicks can be combined with various types of footwork (You could also do the same thing with striking actions):

1) **Curving right step followed by kick** – in this case you use a curving right step followed immediately by a rear hook kick.

2) Curving left step followed by kick – in this case you use a curving left step followed immediately by lead side kick.

3) Pivot right followed by kick – in this case you use a right pivot followed immediately by a lead inverted hook kick.

4) **Pivot left followed by kick** – in this case you use a left pivot, followed immediately by a lead side kick.

5) **Pivot to opposite direction followed by kick** – in this case you pivot to face the opposite direction, followed immediately by lead front thrust kick.

THE KICKING SHIELD

Working Various Attacks Following Retreat

In combat, a fighter needs to possess the ability to switch rapidly from offense to defense and vice versa. The following training methods can help you to develop your ability to hit following some form of retreating action. The feeder advances towards you to simulate some form of attacking action such as a kick or punch. The training partner reacts by using some form of footwork to retreat, then immediately fires their own attack. The following are examples illustrating offensive actions that follow a defensive footwork action:

a) **Push shuffle retreat (same lead) – return kick** – use a quick push shuffle retreat followed immediately by a side kick.

b) **Push shuffle retreat (same lead) – return hand** – use a quick push shuffle retreat followed immediately by a low lead straight punch.

c) **Slide step retreat (same lead) – return kick** – use a slide-step retreat followed immediately by a lead hook kick.

d) Slide-step retreat (same lead) -- return knee -- use a slide-step retreat followed immediately by a vertical rear knee.

e) Step thru retreat (switch leads) – return kick – use a step-thru retreat which switches your lead followed immediately by a rear hook kick.

f) **Step thru retreat (switch leads) – return hand** – use a step-thru retreat which switches your lead, followed immediately by a low rear straight punch.

Combining Various Weapons and Different Ranges

When working out with the shield, you should develop not only your ability to combine various weapons, but also your ability to instantaneously shift from one range or distance to another as the situation demands. The following examples illustrate the use of combining various weapons and adjusting to changing ranges:

a) **Long-range to close-range (Kicking to kneeing)** – Close the distance using a lead hook kick, follow with a rear vertical upward knee. *(See photos below and on next page.)*

THE KICKING SHIELD

b) Long-range to medium range (Kicking to punching) – Close the distance using a lead front thrust kick, follow with a low lead straight punch, low rear cross.

c) Medium-range to close-range (Punching to kneeing) - Feint a rear cross to the head, follow with a lead horizontal inward knee.

d) Medium-range to long-range (punching to kicking) – Hit with a low rear cross, follow with a slide-step lead hook kick as trainer retreats.

e) Close-range to long-range (Kneeing to kicking) – Hit with a lead vertical knee, follow with a rear hook kick as trainer retreats

Kicking from Ground Position

In addition to training your standing kicking and striking skills, the shield can be used to develop your ability to defend yourself and fight from a position on the ground against a standing opponent until you are able to return to standing (if that's your goal). The following examples illustrate how you can train kicking while on the ground:

1) Lead side kick to shin, instep

2) Lead front thrust to knee

 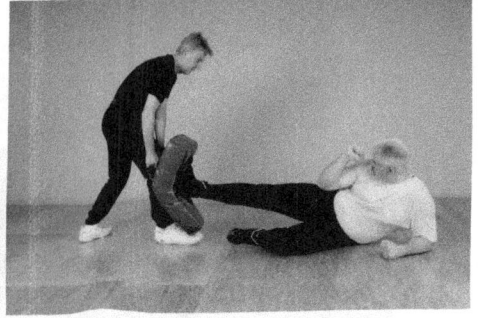

3) Lead front thrust to face

4) Rear oblique kick to shin, instep

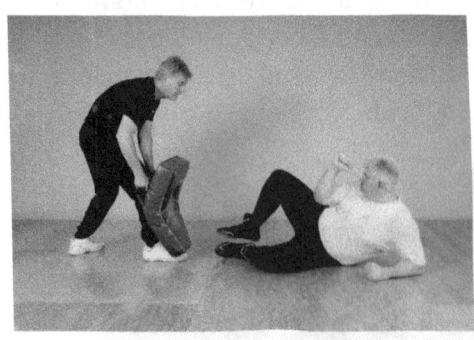

5) Hook Kick to knee, groin

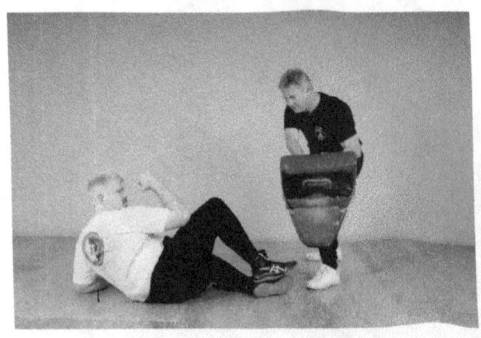

On any of the above actions, the holder can either remain stationary so that the person hitting the shield can develop placement of the kick and proper body-mechanics, or move around and advance toward the person so that they can develop proper timing and distance.

Kicking to Different Directions

In an actual combative situation, an attack may not always come from directly in front of you, or when you're well-prepared and in a ready position. So, it's vital that you learn not only kick in different directions (to the side, behind, etc.) but also be able to explode with a kick from a relaxed, natural position. The following examples illustrate how you can practice kicking in various directions. Some are shown from a fighting stance while others are shown from a relaxed, standing position.

1) Side kick to right side – From a relaxed position, fire a side kick to the right as the person holding the shield takes a step toward you.

2) Rear spin kick to right side – As you are in the midst of walking, fire a spin kick to the right as the holder takes a step toward you.

3) Rear hook kick to left side – From a right-lead ready position, fire a rear hook kick to the left as the holder steps toward you.

4) Rear front thrust to left side -- From a right-lead ready position, fire a rear forward thrust to the left kick as the holder steps toward you.

5) Right back kick (front foot position) -- From a right-lead ready position, fire a lead leg back kick behind you as the holder steps toward you.

6) Left back kick (rear foot position) -- From a right-lead ready position, fire a rear leg back kick behind you as the holder steps toward you.

Additional Use for the Kicking Shield

In addition to striking, the shield can be used to practice certain grappling skills such as shooting in to grappling position and hitting the shield with the shoulder.

Training Tips for Using the Kicking Shield

When you're training someone with the shield, don't just stand still and hold it like some kind of mannequin. Keep the training as alive and realistic as possible. Be a moving target and use your footwork to advance, retreat, and circle the person working on the shield. Change the distance from long to close and vice versa and set different target lines. Make your partner workout and feel as if he is really relating his actions to a real opponent.

CHAPTER THREE

Forearm Pads

Another very useful form of mobile training equipment are the forearm pads; a set of thick, protective pads that run the length of the forearm (sometimes longer). Commonly referred to as "Thai pads" because they originated in Thailand and are used extensively in the training of Muay Thai (Thai Boxing), the forearm pads are an excellent training tool for not only helping you develop your kicking, kneeing, elbowing speed and power, but also helping build high levels of endurance. As with other training equipment, there are various types of forearm pads available on the market today. Some are made for people with longer forearms, others have thicker padding to offer more protection against very powerful strikes. Find the type that best fits you and suits your training needs. Again, I use several types for different purposes.

While the forearm pads are most often used in a pair, they may also be used either singly or combined with a focus glove or even a boxing glove. Many of the same training exercises shown in the Focus Glove chapter on can also be incorporated into training with Thai pads, so you should cross-reference the chapters.

Methods of Using Pads

a) Using two pads

b) Combining forearm pad and focus glove

c) Combining forearm pad and Boxing glove

Holding the Forearm Pads Correctly

No matter how you choose to use the forearm pads (kicking, kneeing, punching, etc.), they should still be held correctly and safely by the trainer. The following examples illustrate of some common mistakes people make when holding them:

a) **Palms facing inwards** – Although this is not an inviolable rule, when training with a very powerful striker, holding the pads with your palms facing inwards puts your arms in a weaker position and opens the possibility of injury to forearm. I remember hearing about a student training in Muay Thai who, after failing to heed the instructor's repeated advice not to hold the pads with his palms facing inward, ended up with a broken forearm.

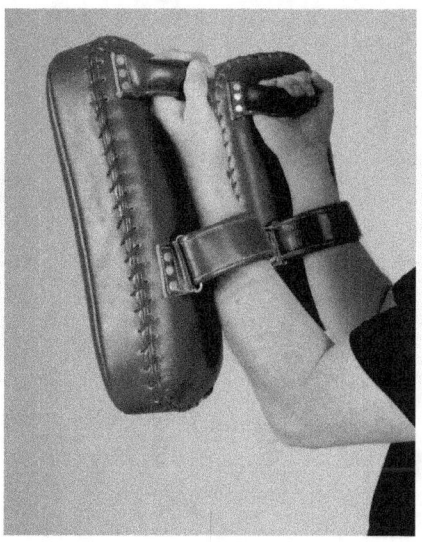

b) Pads held too far away from body – If you hold the pads too far away from your body (or holds your arms too straight) they have very little support against a powerful strike.

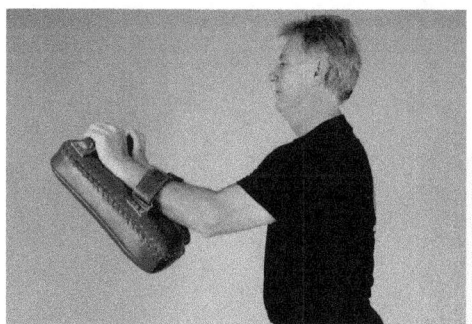

c) Pads held at the wrong angle – If you hold the pads at the wrong angle there is a possibility that a kick or strike may slide off the pads and hit you.

d) Pads held too far apart – If you hold the pads too far apart it can cause the person striking them to develop wide, uneco-nomical motions.

In addition, if you have the pads strapped too tight on your arms you'll have difficulty getting them off quickly by yourself if you need to, and if they are too loose they will move around too much. So, experiment to find the proper fit for yourself.

Various Weapons of Attack

The following photographs illustrate the various striking weapons that can be trained on the Thai pads:

a) Kicking (single actions)

1) Lead upward snap kick

2) Rear upward snap kick

3) Lead front thrust kick to body

4) Lead hook kick

5) Rear hook kick

6) Inverted hook kick

7) Heel hook kick

8) Rear spin kick

9) Rear inward crescent kick

10) Lead outward crescent kick

b) Punching (single actions)

1) Lead straight

2) Rear straight

3) Lead high hook

4) Rear high hook

FOREARM PADS

5) Lead body hook

6) Rear body hook

7) Lead shovel hook

8) Rear shovel hook

9) Lead uppercut

10) Rear uppercut

11) Rear overhand

12) Lead palm hook

13) Rear palm hook

14) Backfist

c) Kneeing (single actions)

1) Lead vertical knee – medium-range

2) Rear vertical knee – medium-range

3) Lead vertical knee -- close-range with tie-up

4) Rear vertical knee -- close-range with tie-up

d) Elbowing (single actions)

1) Lead horizontal inward

2) Rear horizontal inward

FOREARM PADS

3) Lead diagonal upward

4) Rear diagonal upward

5) Lead diagonal downward

6) Rear diagonal downward

7) Lead vertical upward

8) Rear vertical upward

9) Lead vertical downward

10) Rear vertical downward

FOREARM PADS

11) Lead horizontal outward

12) Rear horizontal outward

e) Other (forearm, etc.)

1) Lead inward forearm smash

2) Rear inward forearm smash

FOREARM PADS

3) Lead outward forearm smash

4) Rear outward smash

Training Various Ways of Attack

The following examples illustrate how the various ways of attack such as Attack by Combination, Progressive Indirect Attack, etc. can be trained using the forearm pads. Single Direct Attack has not been included because they were shown in the above section.

Attack by Combination

1) **Foot-Foot** – slide up lead front upward snap kick, drop foot and immediately fire lead hook kick with same leg (feeder remains stationary)

2) **Foot – Foot** – slide up lead inverted hook kick, plant forward and slide up lead hook kick (feeder use slide-step retreat).

FOREARM PADS

3) **Foot-Foot** – slide up lead hook kick, plant forward and fire rear hook kick (feeder use step-thru retreat).

4) **Foot-Hand** -- slide up lead hook kick, plant forward and lead backfist. *(See photos below and on next page.)*

5) **Foot-Hand** – slide up lead upward snap kick, plant forward and lead straight punch to midsection.

6) **Foot-Hand** – slide up front thrust kick, plant forward and lead straight punch high.

FOREARM PADS

7) **Hand – Foot** – High lead straight punch, low rear cross, slide up with lead hook kick as feeder retreats and sets line.

8) **Hand-Foot** – Rear uppercut, high lead hook, rear hook kick as feeder retreats and sets line.

9) **Foot – Knee** – Slide up lead hook kick, plant forward and rear vertical upward knee. *(See photos below and on next page.)*

FOREARM PADS

10) **Hand-Knee** – High lead straight punch, high rear cross, slide up lead vertical upward knee as feeder retreats and sets line.

11) **Hand-Knee** – High lead straight punch, high lead hook, rear horizontal inward knee. *(See photos below and on next page.)*

193

12) **Hand-Elbow** – High lead straight punch, lead uppercut, rear horizontal elbow.

13) **Hand-Elbow** – flow from straight blast punching into rear diagonal upward elbow, followed by high lead elbow hook.

14) **Elbow-Elbow** – Rear diagonal upward elbow, lead horizontal inward elbow, rear diagonal downward elbow.

15) **Elbow-Knee** – lead elbow hook followed by rear vertical upward knee.

16) **Elbow-Forearm** – lead horizontal inward elbow followed by a lead outward forearm smash.

FOREARM PADS

17) **Knee-Elbow** – rear vertical upward knee followed by lead elbow hook, rear horizontal elbow.

18) **Forearm-Elbow** – lead inward forearm smash followed by a rear horizontal elbow. *(See photos below and on next page.)*

Progressive Indirect Attack

1) **Foot-Foot** – feint a low lead front upward snap kick as you close the distance, shift to a high lead hook kick.

2) **Foot-Hand** – feint a low lead hook kick as you close the distance, shift to a high lead backfist. *(See photos below and on next page.)*

3) **Hand-Hand** – feint a low lead straight punch to close the distance, shift to a high lead hook.

4) **Hand-Hand** – feint a high lead straight punch to close the distance, shift to a high rear cross.

5) **Hand-Elbow** – feint a high lead hook punch as you close the distance, shift to a high rear diagonal elbow.

6) **Knee-Hand** – slide up and feint the lead vertical upward knee as you close the distance, shift into a straight blast.

7) **Elbow-Knee** – feint a lead elbow hook as you close the distance with footwork, shift to a rear vertical knee.

Attack by Drawing

1) Lower your lead arm to draw the opponent's rear straight punch at your face, which you parry and strike with a rear vertical upward knee.

2) Lower your rear arm to draw opponent's lead hook punch at your head, which you intercept with a rear inside straight punch to the face.

3) Feint using a backward step to draw the opponent to step forward, then hit him with a low lead hook kick as he is in the midst of moving.

Combining Offensive/Defensive Skills

As combat is fluid and can change from moment to moment, it's important in your training to practice shifting from offense to defense and vice versa. The following examples illustrate how you can practice shifting from attack to defense and defense to counterattack using the forearm pads.

Shifting from Offense to Defense

1) Close the distance with a lead hook kick to the pad, bob and weave to escape under the trainer's high lead hook punch aimed at your head. *(See photos below and on next page.)*

2) Close the distance with your lead upward front snap kick to the pad, slip outside the trainer's lead jab to your face.

3) Fire mid-level rear hook kick to the pads, use a shin cover against the trainer's low rear kick aimed at your thigh.

FOREARM PADS

4) Hit with your lead straight punch to the pad, then snap away from the trainer's high rear straight punch at your face.

5) Hit with your high rear straight punch to the pad, use a left forearm cover against the trainer's right hook to your body.

6) Hit with your rear diagonal downward elbow to the pad, shoulder roll away from the trainer's rear straight punch to your face.

7) Hit the pads with a rear vertical upward knee, then use a push shuffle retreat step to evade the trainer's rear straight punch aimed at your body.

Shifting from Defense to Offense

1) Evade the trainer's low lead hook kick using retreating footwork, hit with lead straight, rear straight, lead hook punching combination as trainer recovers forward. *(See photos below and on next page.)*

2) In unmatched leads, use a step-through retreat to evade the trainer's rear hook at your thigh, blast a rear hook kick to the stomach.

3) Evade the trainer's rear oblique kick aimed at your lead leg by lifting it, drop it back down and immediately return a lead straight, rear overhand, lead shovel hook punch combination.

4) Slip outside the trainer's lead straight punch at your face, then fire a rear shovel hook to the body.

5) Use a shin cover against the trainer's low hook kick to your thigh or groin, fire a lead backfist, rear cross, lead elbow combination.

FOREARM PADS

6) Duck underneath the trainer's lead hook at your head and fire a lead and rear straight punch to the groin.

7) Snap away from the trainer's lead straight punch, return "straight blast." *(See photos below and on next page.)*

8) Use a rear forearm deflection against the trainer's straight punch to your body, fire lead horizontal elbow, rear vertical upward knee.

Developing Good Timing

As with the focus gloves and kicking shield, you can develop your ability to time an opponent by hitting the pads when the trainer gives you some form of visual or auditory "cue". The goal is to work on increasing your speed of seeing the signal or cue and reducing the time it takes for you to react to it. The following examples illustrate various visual cues that can be used:

1) Hit with a one-two punching combination as the trainer drops or lowers his lead arm.

2) Lead hook kick to the midsection as the trainer raises his rear elbow.

3) Rear hook kick to the midsection as the trainer quick switches his lead.

4) Lead hook kick as the trainer steps forward (kick should land before the trainer completes his forward movement.

FOREARM PADS

5) Lead hook kick as the trainer steps backward (kick should land before the trainer completes his backward movement)

6) Inverted hook kick to the midsection as the trainer uses a step-through retreat to open the distance.

7) Spinning side thrust kick to stomach as trainer takes a sidestep.

Kicking/Striking from Ground Position

The forearm pads can also be used to develop your ability to strike from a position on the ground. The trainer can remain either standing and feed various lines or set targets while on the ground himself. The following examples illustrate various methods of striking from a ground position:

FOREARM PADS

1) Hook kick (trainer standing)

2) Front thrust kick (trainer standing)

3) Heel hook kick (trainer standing)

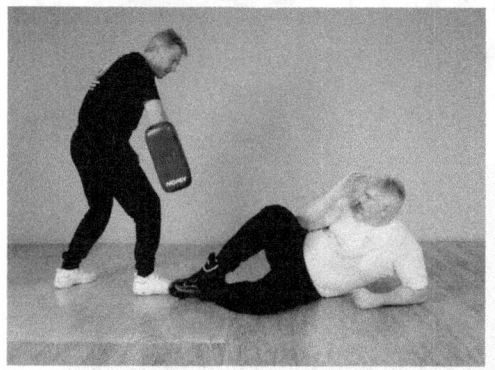

4) Elbow (trainer in mounted position)

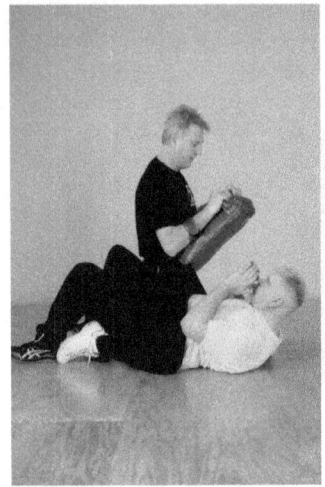

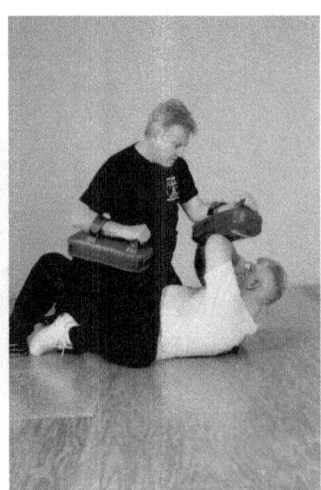

5) Elbow (trainer in bottom position)

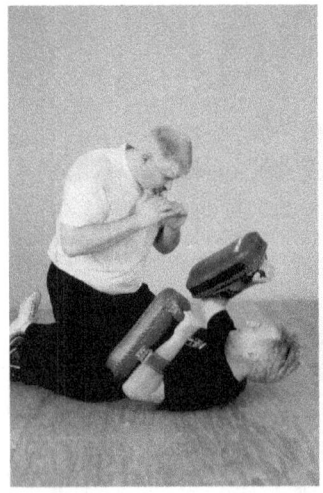
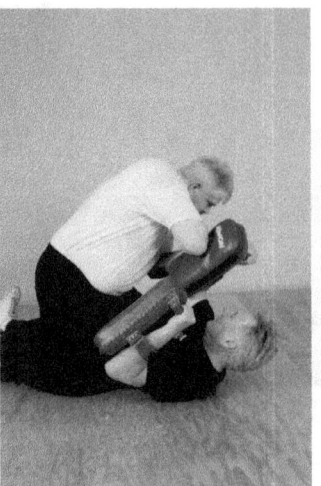
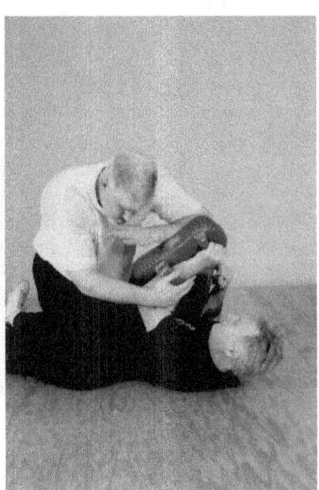

Conclusion

Many of the same drills illustrated in the chapter of focus glove training such as the "Hit and Set Drill," "Set and then Hit Drill," as well as the use of feints and false attacks can and should be used when working with the forearm pads. Again, you're only limited by your own imagination in developing different routines. Just remember to maintain the integrity of the training drill.

CHAPTER FOUR

The Heavy Bag

The heavy bag is referred to as "fixed" equipment because, unlike the focus gloves, kicking shield, or forearm pads that can be carried with you wherever you go, a heavy bag remains primarily in one location. However, unlike focus gloves, kicking shield, or forearm pads, a heavy bag doesn't require the assistance of a partner in order to be able to use it. Nowadays, heavy bags are made out of a variety of materials (canvas, vinyl, leather, etc.) and come in a variety of shapes, lengths, and weights. Besides using the normal size heavy bag (approx. 70 lbs.), Bruce Lee also trained on a custom-built heavy bag that weighed 300 pounds in order to develop even greater striking power. According to Dan Inosanto, Lee would swing the huge bag until it was parallel to the ground, then stand in front of it and stop the bag dead in its tracks with a single kick. Lee's reasoning was that if he could stop the giant bag with a kick, then he could knock a 300-pound opponent on his behind.

The heavy bag is one of the most important and essential pieces of training equipment in any martial artist's equipment arsenal, and can be used to develop a multitude of essential qualities such as power, timing, rhythm, accuracy, balance, proper recovery, etc. You can use the heavy bag for not only developing devastating power in your kicks and strikes but learning to apply that power properly as well. Power can be defined as, "the ability to release an explosive force to produce a quick, sudden movement to move the body with maximum effort." In any form of kicking or striking, the arm or leg is merely the vehicle you use to express the force of your entire body. Power in kicking and striking comes from correct contact of the combative tool at the right spot at the right moment with the body in perfect alignment and well-balanced; not from the preparation beforehand or the vigor with which the blow is thrown. In addition to teaching proper placement of your combative weapons, the heavy bag can help you learn how to coordinate the various parts of your body (leg, waist, arm, etc.) into a coherent and dynamic whole in order to generate maximum power.

Lack of body torque -- In this example, the person hitting the bag with a lead hook punch is only using his arm to hit with, which results in the blow having a lack of power.

Correct body torque – In this example, the person has combined the torque from his leg, waist, shoulder and arm to generate maximum power in the punch.

The heavy bag can also be an invaluable tool for developing your sense of timing. Many people mistakenly believe that strength and weight are the prime ingredients for hard hitting. While both of these physical attributes are useful and may play a role in a person's power, the real secret of powerful hitting and kicking lies not in strength or weight, but rather in accurate timing of the blow. That's why you sometimes see a smaller fighter who seems to hit like a mule and has amazing knockout power. You can use the heavy bag help develop your ability to strike at the right moment and at the proper distance to deliver the most powerful blow you're capable of generating.

Finally, the heavy bag can be used to practice unleashing a barrage of rapid-fire, non-stop heavy blows, with the idea being to keep an opponent off-balance and prevent them from recovering or countering.

"Bags Don't Hit Back"

A major training principle to keep in mind when working on the heavy bag is since the bag doesn't hit back, you don't have to be concerned of potential counterattacks, such as when you're working with a partner using focus gloves. If you're not careful, this can make it easy for you to become sloppy with your actions. You can become careless and either take too much time preparing your strikes and kicks, neglect proper defensive coverage and leave yourself open or uncovered while hitting or kicking it, or forget about quick recovery after your actions. So the idea when using a heavy bag is to fight it in the same manner as you would a real opponent who also has the potential to hit you if you make mistakes. Make sure to keep yourself well-covered and protected at all times. Use all types of footwork such as advancing, retreating and sidestepping to move in, out and around the bag as you are working it. Combine the use of feints and false attacks as well as broken rhythm as you vary and combine your kicks, punches, elbow and knee strikes to the bag. Don't shove or flick at the bag, but rather, focus on the target and "explode" through it with your strikes. Above all, think of economical motions when you train.

Protect Your Hands

When hitting the heavy bag hard, especially if you're going to be working out for multiple rounds or for an extended period of time (such as 15-30 minutes, etc.), you should wrap your hands in order to protect the bones in both the hand and the wrist. The reason for this is the longer you train, the more tired you become, and the less careful you can become. As a result, the potential for injuries increases. There are numerous ways to wrap your hand. No one method will suit all martial artists, due to individual variations in hand size, bone structure and inherent weaknesses. It's up to you to discover the one that works best for you. You should also learn to wrap your own hands so that you don't have to rely on someone else to wrap them (unless you're preparing for a competition and have a professional trainer that wraps them for you). When you wrap your hands, make sure that your fist and forearm forms a straight line and has no bending at the wrist, as this can lead to potential injury. Also make sure the wraps are not so tight that they cut off blood circulation in your hands, or so loose that they fall off when you are working out. Only you can feel the right degree of tension in the wrap that your hands need.

CORRECT WRAPPING — These photos illustrate the wrist wrapped correctly with wrist straight.

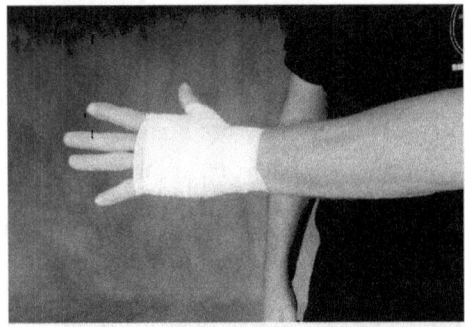
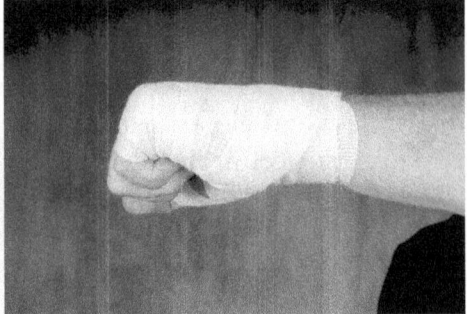

INCORRECT WRAPPING — These photographs illustrate the wrist wrapped incorrectly and bent forward and backward (wrist-bend is exaggerated for clarity).

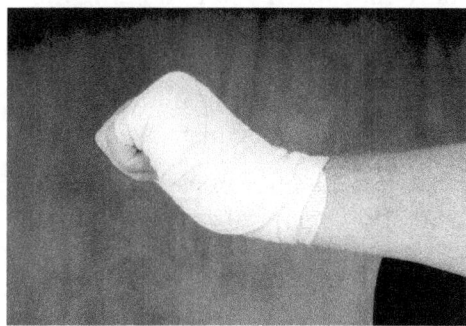
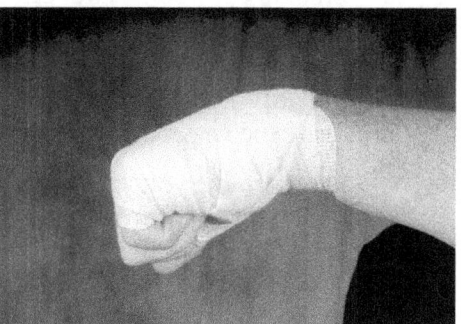

Bag gloves should also be worn over the hand wrappings to prevent the wrappings from slipping off and provide additional protection to the hands. According to Dan Inosanto, while Bruce Lee did wear bag gloves many times when he was punching the heavy bag, he didn't wrap his hands. This was because he felt that in a real fight your hands wouldn't be wrapped and that a person could become too used to having their hand protected when striking. But it's important to remember that Lee spent a great deal of time both developing and strengthening the muscles in his forearms and hands, and conditioning them for actual contact by hitting various types of bags, etc. I recommend that you use some form of hand protection any time you are punching a heavy bag. There are also many types of bag gloves now available that have hand support and wrist wraps already built into them. Again, find what works best for you.

Some people do not like to wrap their hands or wear any form of hand protection because their attitude is that you will not be wearing gloves out on the street. That is their choice. However, if you're working out bag bare-handed and you accidentally hit a seam on the bag, it can tear the skin off your knuckles. Then you have to let it heal or risk tearing it open again every time you work out.

Holding the Heavy Bag

Sometimes you work out on the heavy bag by yourself. At other times you might have a training partner hold the heavy bag for your while you are kicking and striking it. Your partner can not only help stabilize the bag and stop it from swinging all over the place, but also give you verbal feedback on such things as if you are over-preparing or telegraphing your actions, whether your blow exploding properly through the bag or is more of a push or flick, and whether or not you're recovering back to your ready position quickly. There are different ways of holding the heavy bag, and how you do it is a matter of personal preference. Just make sure that when you're holding the bag for your partner, (a) you can control the bag; (b) that you can see the person hitting the bag; and (c) while holding the bag your hands or body aren't vulnerable to being hit. The following photographs illustrate incorrect or unsafe methods of holding the bag:

a) By wrapping your arms too far the bag when holding it, you make them vulnerable to getting hit when the opponent strikes the bag.

b) Standing with your back to the bag not only prevents you from seeing what your partner is doing and when they strike, but can make you vulnerable to neck whiplash or other back injuries if your partner unloads a very powerful kick.

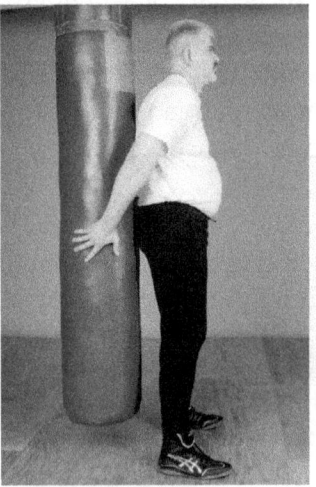 

c) Having your face directly behind the bag blocks your view and prevents you from seeing what the person hitting the bag is doing.

The following photographs illustrate some ways of safely holding the heavy bag:

a) You can hold the bag from behind with your arms slightly extended and the bag away from your body.

b) You can hold the bag from behind with both arms and with it close to your body.

c) You can hold the bag from a right or left side position.

d) You can catch and hold the bag as your partner kicks it backward to prepare it for a follow-up motion (such as lead side kick to rear spin kick).

e) You can also hold the heavy bag upright on the ground so that your partner can practice low-line kicks, which is useful if you do not have a full-length heavy bag. *(See photos on next page.)*

Dividing the Heavy Bag into Sections

To help you train more realistically you can visually break the heavy bag into various sections or target areas (some people actually draw lines or targets on the bag itself). Start with an imaginary vertical line running straight through the center of the bag as you face it. This divides the bag into left and right sides (or inside and outside if you prefer). Next, divide the bag with an imaginary horizontal line running across the middle of the bag, giving you high and middle areas (or head and body sections if you prefer). If you have a long banana bag such as the kind Thai Boxers use, you can also add a third section which would be considered the opponent's legs, or low-line, groin, etc.).

Proper Distance and Depth of Penetration When Striking

When kicking or striking the heavy bag, if you're too close to the bag when you strike it, or your strike penetrates too deeply, the blow will be smothered and become more of a 'push' that will shove an opponent away. On the other hand, if you're too far away or you don't penetrate deep enough with your strike, the blow will turn into more of a 'flick' that will do little or no damage to the opponent. By maintaining proper distance from the bag and aiming your blow several inches through the target you'll achieve proper depth of penetration with your blows.

a) Too deep -- By penetrating too deeply with the lead straight punch, the blow becomes more of a "shove" than a hit. *(See photo on next page.)*

b) Too shallow – By not penetrating deeply enough with the lead straight punch, the blow becomes more of a "flick."

Working Various Distances

There are three primary distances or ranges you can work at when training on the heavy bag; (a) long-range, (b) medium-range, and (c) close-range. The following photographs illustrate the various distances in relation to the bag:

THE HEAVY BAG

a) **Long-range** – This distance is primarily used for kicking

b) **Medium range** – At this distance various kicks, punches, and elbow strikes can be used.

c) **Close-range** – At this distance, tight hook and uppercut punches, elbow and knee strikes, as well as other close quarter fighting tools such as shoulder-butting and even head-butting can be used. *(See photo on next page.)*

The following examples illustrate how you can shift between the various ranges when working on the bag:

1) **Long-range to Medium-range** — Close the distance using a slide-step lead side kick, then plant the leg forward and hit with a lead backfist.

2) **Long-range to Close-range** — Close the distance with a slide-step lead hook kick, feint a lead finger jab and shoot in and hit the bag with a lead shoulder butt to simulate moving into grappling.
   (See photos on following page)

3) Medium-range to Close-range — Fire a lead straight punch, followed by a lead hook, rear horizontal elbow, rear vertical knee.

The Various Weapons of Attack

The following photographs illustrate the various combative tools that you can train on the heavy bag:

HANDS:

1) Lead straight punch with vertical fist (high)

2) Lead straight punch with horizontal fist (high)

3) Lead straight punch with horizontal fist (low)

4) Lead backfist (high)

5) Lead backfist (low)

6) Lead hook (high)

7) Lead hook (low)

THE HEAVY BAG

8) Lead shovel hook

9) Lead corkscrew hook

10) Lead palm hook (high)

11) Lead palm hook (low)

12) Lead uppercut

13) Lead straight punch with half-knuckle fist

14) Rear straight (high)

15) Rear straight (low)

16) Rear hook (high)

17) Rear hook (low)

18) Rear shovel hook

19) Rear uppercut

20) Rear overhand (corkscrew)

21) Rear palm hook (high)

22) Rear palm hook (low)

23) Rear palm smash (straight on)

24) The "Straight Blast"

FEET:

1) Lead upward snap kick

NOTE: *When working the upward snap kick it is better to use a smaller heavy bag as opposed to the full-length bag used here so you can hit the bottom of it.*

2) Lead thrust kick

3) Lead hook kick

4) Lead side kick

5) Lead inverted hook kick

6) Lead heel hook kick

7) Lead outward crescent kick

8) Lead inward crescent kick

9) Rear upward snap kick

10) Rear front thrust kick

11) Rear hook kick

12) Rear spinning back kick

13) Rear heel hook kick

14) Rear inward crescent kick

15) Rear outward crescent kick

16) Rear back kick

TRAINING NOTE —If you don't have a full-length heavy bag, a regular-size bag can also be held upright on the ground by your partner or stood upright in a room corner to allow you to practice your low-line shin/knee kicks against it.

ELBOWS:

1) Lead horizontal inward (high)

2) Lead horizontal inward (low)

3) Lead diagonal upward

4) Lead vertical upward

5) Lead horizontal outward (illustrates lead outward elbow following a hook punch)

6) Rear horizontal inward (high)

7) Rear horizontal inward (low)

8) Rear diagonal upward

9) Rear diagonal downward

10) Rear vertical upward

11) Rear horizontal outward (illustrates rear outward elbow following a hook punch).

12) Backward (high)

13) Backward (low)

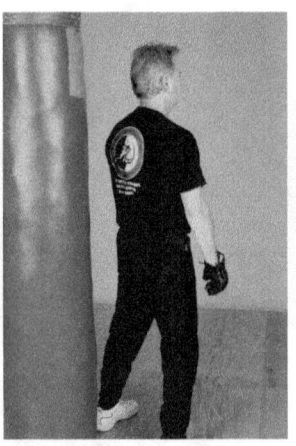 

KNEES:

1) Vertical upward (lead)

THE HEAVY BAG

2) Vertical upward (rear)

3) Horizontal inward (lead)

4) Horizontal inward (rear)

FOREARM:

1) Inside forearm smash

2) Outside forearm smash

SHOULDER BUTT:

HEADBUTT:

Training Various Ways of Attack:

Offensive combinations can be created using two, three, four, or even more actions. When combined with other things such as feints and false attacks, the number of potential combinations you can create is endless. The following examples illustrate how different methods of attack can be trained on the heavy bag:

1. Attack by Combination (ABC)

a) **Foot-Foot** – slide-step lead upward snap kick to lead hook kick

b) Foot-Foot – slide-step lead side kick to rear spin kick

c) Foot-Hand – slide-step lead hook kick to lead backfist

d) Foot-Hand – slide-step lead inverted hook kick to low lead straight

e) Hand-Hand – high lead straight punch, lead shovel hook, rear high hook.

f) Hand-Elbow – low lead straight punch, high lead hook, rear diagonal elbow.

g) Hand-Knee – high lead backfist, high rear cross, rear vertical upward knee.

h) Hand-Forearm – lead uppercut, rear uppercut, lead forearm smash.

i) Elbow-Knee – rear horizontal elbow, lead horizontal elbow, rear vertical upward knee.

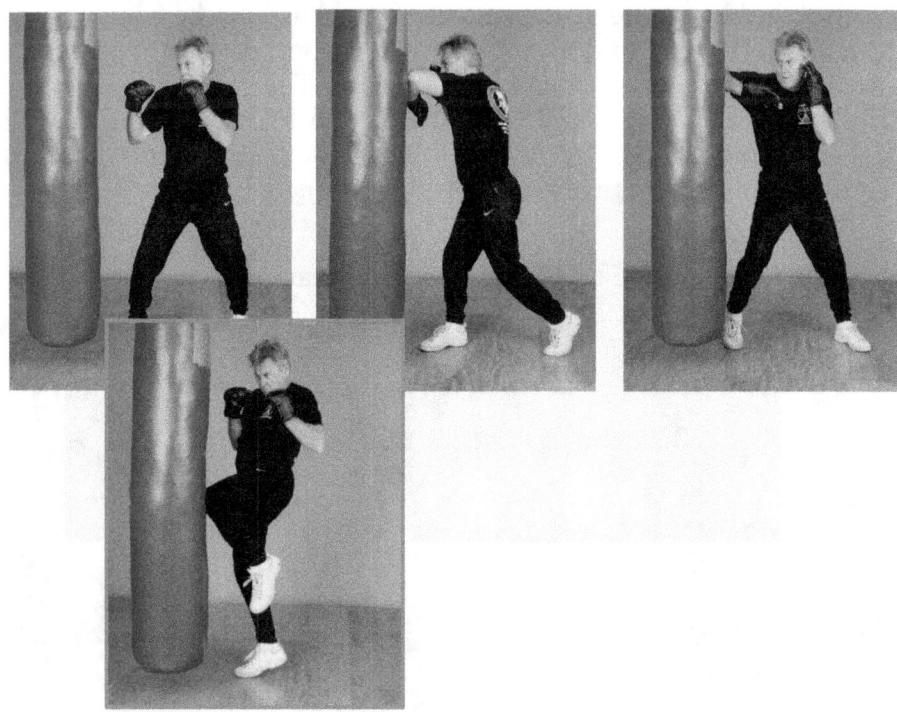

j) Knee-Elbow – lead vertical knee, lead hooking elbow, rear diagonal upward elbow.

Use of Feints/False Attacks in ABC

Remember that when using a combination or compound attack, not all of the blows have to score. Some of the blows may be feints or false attacks designed to draw a defensive reaction or open a particular line for the next or final blow to score. The following examples illustrate how feints and false attacks can be used when training combination attacks on the heavy bag. (Note the difference between these combinations and the following section on Progressive Indirect Attack):

1) Feint a high lead backfist, hit with low rear cross

2) Feint a low lead straight punch, hit with a high rear cross or overhand.

3) Feint a high lead hook, hit with a diagonal rear elbow.

4) Feint a high lead elbow hook, hit with rear vertical knee.

5) Feint a low lead straight punch, hit with high rear hook kick.

6) Use a body drop feint followed by a high lead hook kick

7) Feint a rear leg oblique kick followed by a rear overhand punch.

2. Progressive Indirect Attack (PIA)

As I explained in the previous chapters, the primary difference between Attack By Combination and Progressive Indirect Attack is that, while ABC can be done either moving or stationary, PIA involves closing the distance to the opponent in a progressive, forward-flowing movement. The following examples illustrate training PIA on the bag:

a) **Foot-Foot** – use a low lead front kick feint to close the distance, then shift to a high lead hook kick.

b) **Foot-Hand** – use a low lead hook kick to close the distance, then shift to a high lead straight punch.

c) **Hand-Hand** – use a low lead straight punch to close the distance, then shift to a high lead backfist.

d) **Hand-Elbow** -- use a high lead palm hook to close the distance, then shift to a rear diagonal down elbow.

e) **Hand – Knee** –use a high lead backfist to close the distance, then shift to a lead vertical upward knee.

f) **Knee-Elbow** – use a lead vertical upward knee to close the distance, then shift to a rear horizontal elbow.

g) **Elbow-Knee** – use a lead elbow hook to close the distance, then shift to a rear vertical upward knee.

3. Attack by Drawing (ABD)

Attack by Drawing consists of using some form of 'bait' or 'lure' (such as intentionally opening a line, or using footwork such as a quick advance or retreat) to draw an offensive or counter-offensive reaction from an opponent, which you then use to complete your own attack. As the heavy bag cannot strike at you, when practicing ABD you'll have to make proper use of your imagination in visualizing how an opponent reacts to your initial drawing action in order to work your follow-up action. The following examples illustrate training Attack by Drawing on the heavy bag:

1. Lower your lead arm to draw the opponent's lead or rear straight punch into the now-open line, lean away and hook kick.

2. Lower your lead arm to draw the opponent's lead or rear straight punch into the now-open line, sidestep outside and hit with a high lead hook.

3. Lower your rear arm to draw the opponent's hooking attack into the now-open line, bob forward and hit with a rear overhand.

4. Lower your rear arm to draw opponent's hooking attack into the now-open line, shift sideways and hook kick the bag with your rear leg.

5. Slip inside an opponent's lead punch to draw his rear straight punch, counter with a lead hook to the head as you shoulder roll away.

4. Hand Immobilization Attack (HIA)

As with Attack by Drawing, by visualizing an opponent's arms and their actions or reactions, it's possible to train certain Hand Immobilization Attacks on the heavy bag. The following examples illustrate how you can practice some of the various HIA actions with a heavy bag:

1. Use a low lead straight punch to draw the opponent's lead hand downward block, which you trap with a slapping hand trap (pak sao) and score with a lead backfist.

2. Use a high lead straight punch to draw the opponent's lead hand inward block, which you trap with a slapping hand trap (pak sao) and score score with a lead backfist.

3. Use a high lead straight punch to draw the opponent's lead hand outward block, which you trap with a grabbing hand (lop sao) and hit with a high rear straight punch.

Training Methods with a Partner

With the aid of a training partner, you can use the heavy bag to develop or increase your reaction and movement speed. The training partner gives you a visual or auditory signal that you have to respond to with a particular strike (or strikes) as quickly as possible. The objective for the person working on the bag is to reduce the time it takes for them recognize the signal and react. The following are examples of visual and auditory cues that can be used:

1) **Hitting the bag as soon as your partner pulls one hand away** – In this example the person working on the bag fires a lead straight punch the moment the person holding the bag pulls one hand away.

2) **Kicking the bag as soon as your partner lifts one leg** – In this example the person working on the bag fires a rear hook kick the moment the person holding the bag lifts one leg off the ground.

3) **Hitting the bag as soon as your partner (who should be out of your vision) claps his hands together** – In this example the person working on the bag fires a lead hook punch as soon as he hears the sound.

Another way you can train your auditory awareness is to practice striking the bag as soon as you hear a particular pre-recorded auditory cue such as a hand-clap or sticks hitting together.

Methods of Using Heavy Bag Without a Partner

When you are working on the heavy bag by yourself, besides working on your various striking actions, you can use the bag in various ways to develop or enhance specific qualities such as your agility, timing, etc. The following examples illustrate various ways you can use the heavy bag to develop these qualities:

1) You can swing the bag backwards and forward and work on increasing your agility using footwork such as:

   a) advancing/retreating while maintaining a precise distance from the bag.

   b) side-stepping or moving off-line so that you avoid the bag as it swings back towards you. *(See photos on following page.)*

  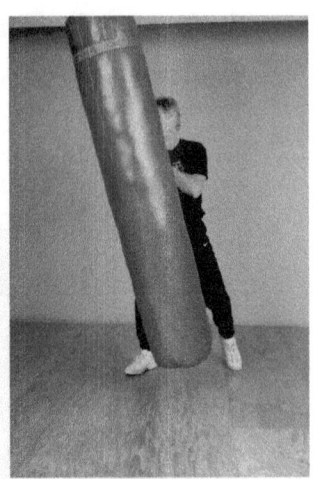

2) You can shove the bag backwards and strike it as it returns to you to time an opponent moving towards you.

3) You can shove the bag backward and hit it as it moves away from you in order to develop penetration against an opponent moving away from you.

4) You can swing the bag sideways and hit it with a punch or kick as it returns to help develop stopping power (Make sure that you hit the bag correctly in order to prevent injury)

As with training with a partner, you can create some form of auditory cue that you have to react to such as using a metronome or making an audiotape with some non-rhythmic noise that you have to react to.

Practicing Grappling Skills with the Heavy Bag

The heavy bag can also be used to practice certain grappling and ground-fighting skills, such as:

1) You can practice working your sprawl position with the bag on the ground and moving around on top of it to simulate moving around on an opponent.

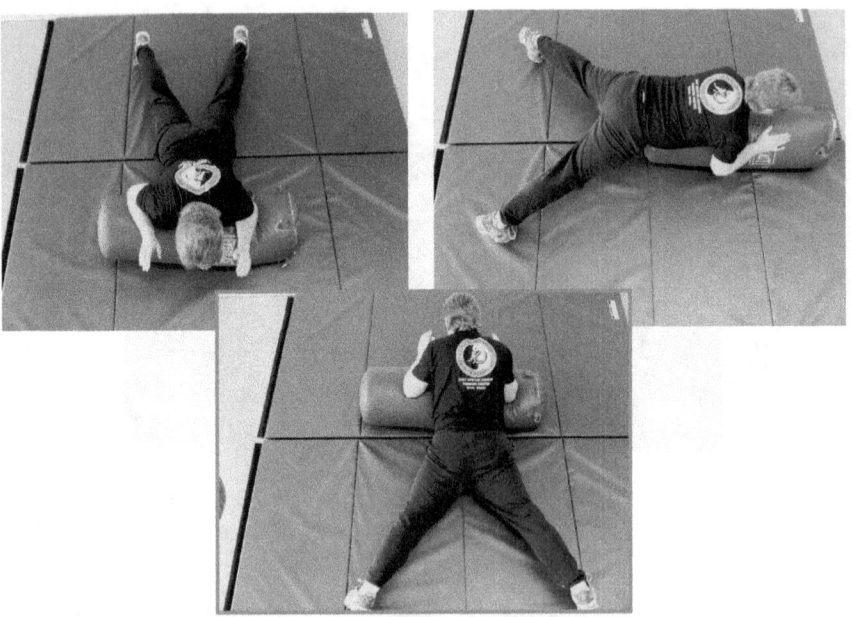

2) You can practice shooting in and lifting the bag from ground as partner holds it upright to simulate shooting in and lifting an opponent.

3) You can practice holding the bag with your legs (guard position) on the ground and practicing various punches and strikes in order to simulate striking an opponent while they're in your guard.

4) You can practice maintaining a knee-on-stomach position while striking the bag to simulate striking an opponent while controlling them on the ground with your knee.

 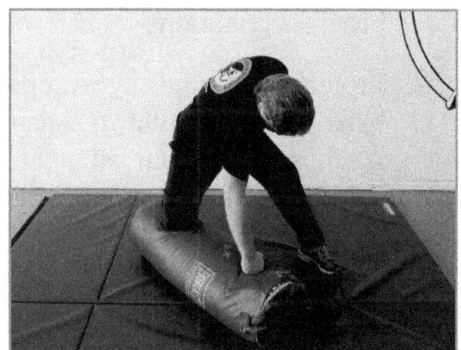

5) You can practice hitting the bag with various strikes while main-taining a sitting position on top of it to simulate striking an opponent while maintaining a mounted position on them.

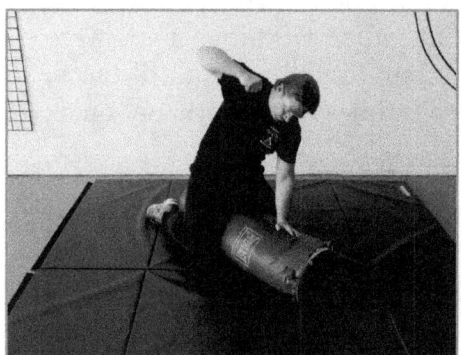 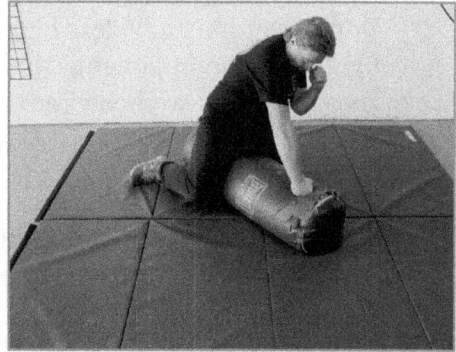

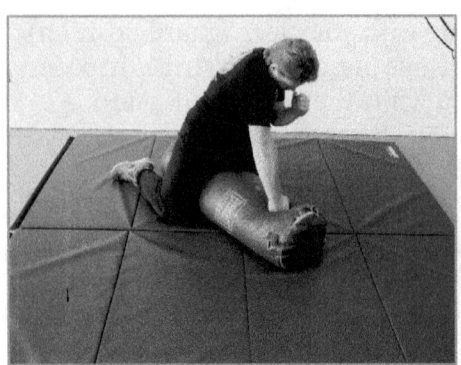 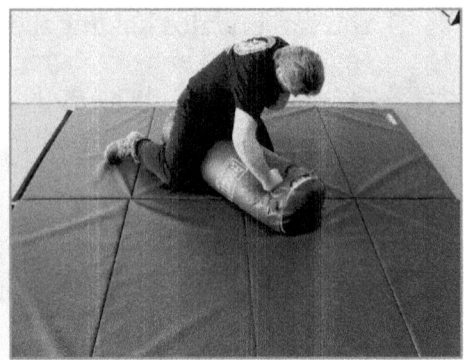

Training Aids for Using the Heavy Bag

1. Remember that the heavy bag has no ego and doesn't feel any pain. Don't try to "kill" the bag or punch it very hard during your initial training sessions or when you first start working out on it each time. Turn up the volume of your various strikes slowly and progress gradually.

2. Protect your hands by wrapping them if you going to hit the bag hard. Make sure that you keep your wrist straight and don't allow it to bend when your fist makes contact with the bag. Make proper contact with whatever striking tool you are using. When punching, keep your hand loose up until the moment of impact on the bag, then tighten it.

3. Relax and gather your strength, then concentrate your mind and all your strength on exploding it through the target. Remember that the arms and legs should express the dynamic force of your entire body.

4. Avoid developing a careless attitude when working on the bag. Don't treat it as a lifeless blob, but rather, fight it as if you were fighting a live opponent. Move around it, adjust your distance, keep yourself well-covered at all times and work on quick recovery after kicking or striking.

5. Hit the bag different ways, or with different degrees of intensity. Sometimes work out on it lightly (but not "powder-puffing"), other times go all-out (but safely)

6. Develop the ability to strike the bag from any angle; high to low, low to high, inside to outside and vice versa.

CHAPTER FIVE
Double-end Bag

The top-and-bottom bag, or double-end bag as it is also called, is a round (or sometimes teardrop-shaped) inflatable target that is supported from the top and bottom by a pair of springy cords which allow it to move back and forth, side to side, and even in circles. As a training tool it is very useful in developing both your footwork and your combination punches and elbow strikes. It also helps you develop distance, timing, and accuracy. The neat thing about the top-and-bottom bag is that it disappears the moment it's hit and rebounds just as fast. So the harder you hit it, the faster it returns, and this keeps you alert. The top-and-bottom bag also helps improve your accuracy by teaching you to hit straight and square, because if you don't hit it correctly, it won't return on the same line, but instead wobble all over the place or swing in circles. The top-and-bottom bag can also be a useful tool in developing your upper body evasive abilities such as slipping and snapping away from punches while still remaining in range to counter. In the same way you train on the heavy bag, the objective when training on the top-and-bottom bag is to fight it as if you were fighting a live opponent, by using your footwork to move around it and control it. Most people use the top-and-bottom bag simply for hitting, but according to Dan Inosanto, Bruce Lee used his legs in the same way as his hands, and would move around the bag and hit it not only with various hand and arm strikes, but also with hook kicks, inverted hook kicks, side kicks, etc. As I stated before, the value of any piece of training equipment lies in the ability and imagination of the person using it.

The Various Weapons

The following examples illustrate the various single combative tools that can be trained on the top-and-bottom bag. Keep in mind that the type of blow used will determine the line the bag returns on. For example, a straight punch will send the bag away from you and back toward you, whereas a hook punch will move the bag laterally left and right in front of you.

a) Hands:

1) Lead straight punch

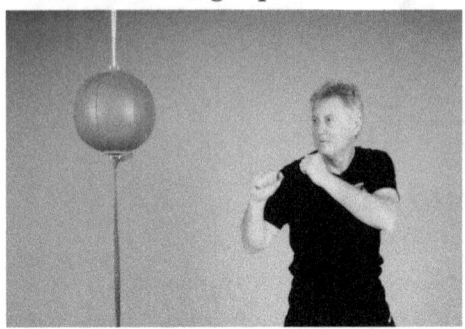
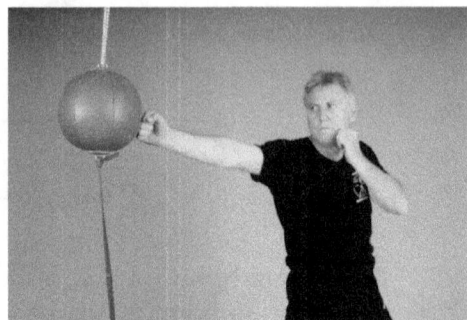

2) Lead backfist

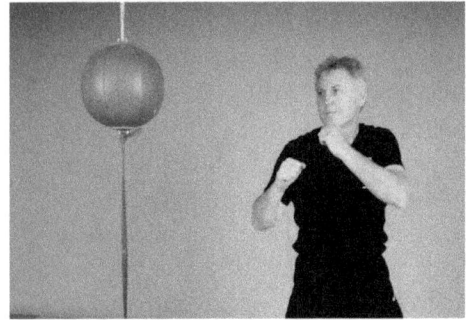

3) Lead hook

4) Lead uppercut

DOUBLE END BAG

5) Lead palm hook

 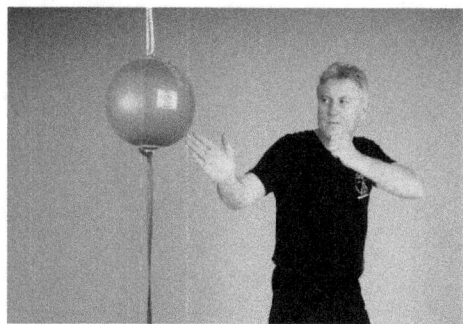

6) Rear straight punch

 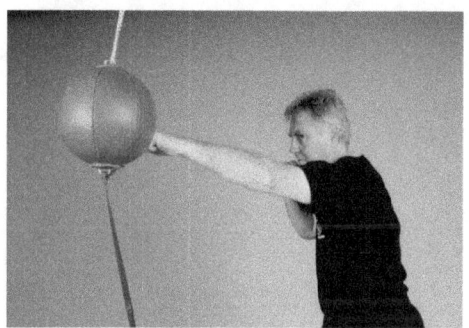

7) Rear overhand

8) Rear hook

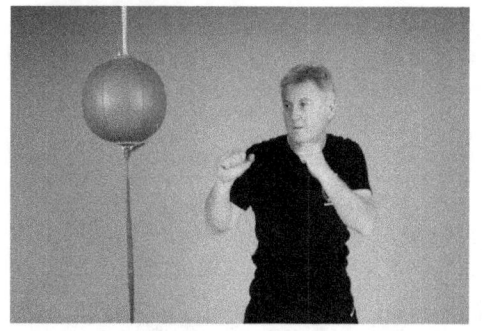 

9) Rear uppercut

10) Rear palm hook

B) Elbows:

1) Lead upward

2) Lead inward

DOUBLE END BAG

3) Lead diagonal downward

4) Lead diagonal upward

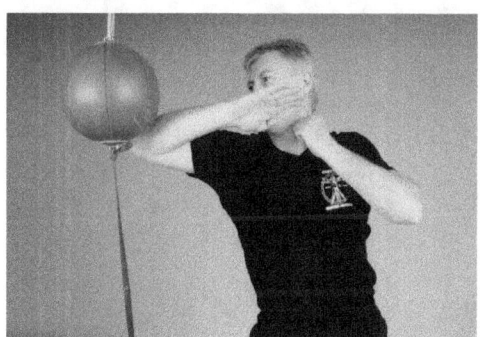

5) Lead outward

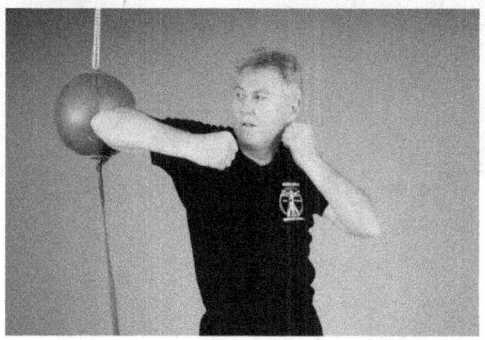

6) Rear upward

7) Rear inward

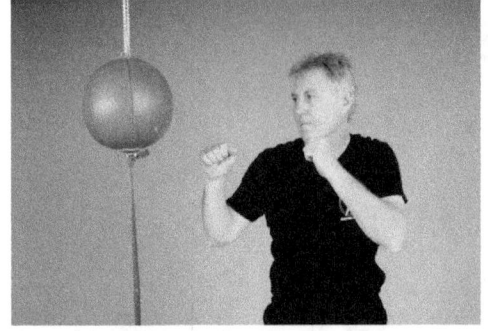 

8) Rear diagonal downward

9) Rear diagonal upward

DOUBLE END BAG

10) Rear outward

C) Feet:

1) Lead hook kick

2) Lead side kick

3) Lead inverted hook kick

4) Lead sweeping kick (heel hook)

5) Rear hook kick

6) Rear inward crescent kick

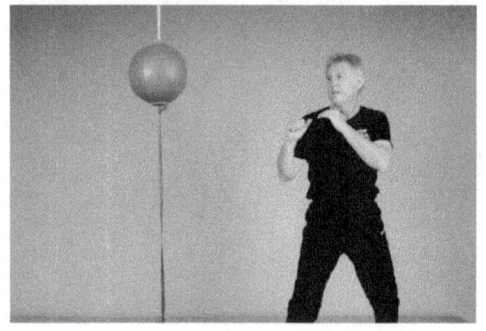 

D) Other Actions:
a) Headbutt

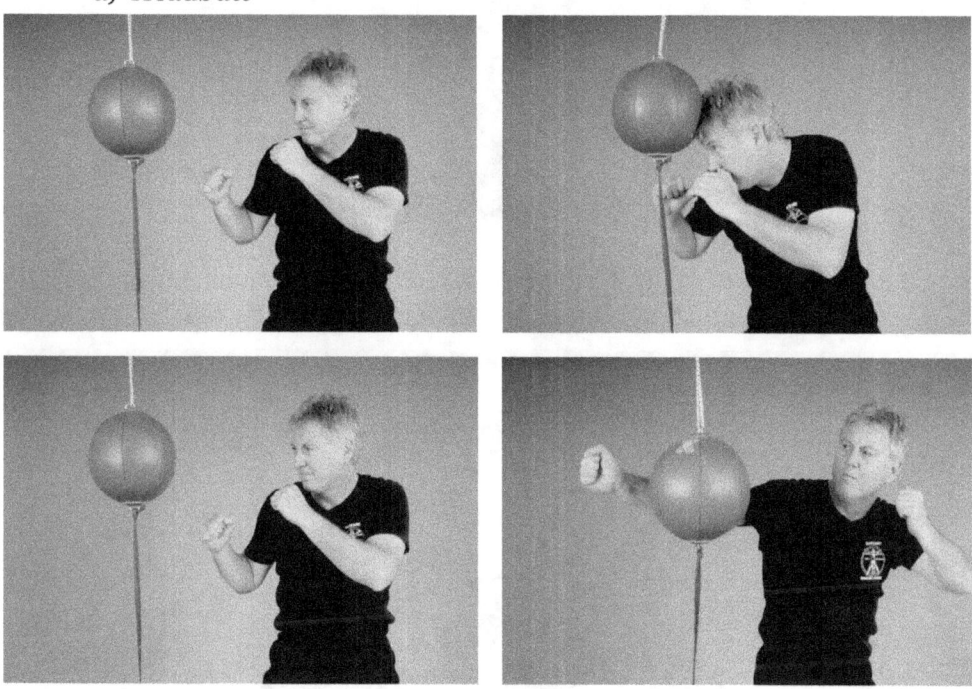

The Five Ways of Attack

While primarily used to practice Single Direct Attack and Attack by Combination, when combined with proper use of your imagination, the top-and-bottom bag can also be used to practice your Progressive Indirect Attack and Attack By Drawing skills. The following examples illustrate combining your various weapons of attack on the top-and-bottom bag:

1. **Hand-Hand** – Hit the bag with a lead straight punch, and as the bag returns towards you, hit it with a lead hook.

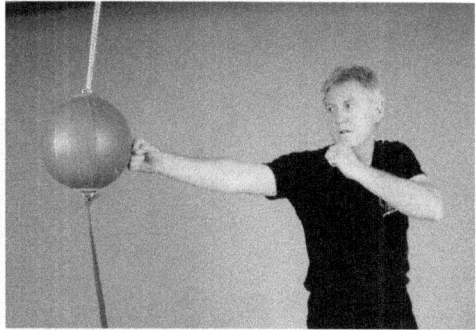

2. Hand-Hand – Hit the bag with a lead straight punch, and as the bag returns towards you, hit it with a rear straight cross.

3. Hand-Elbow – Hit the bag with a lead straight punch, and as the bag returns towards you, hit it with a rear vertical upward elbow.

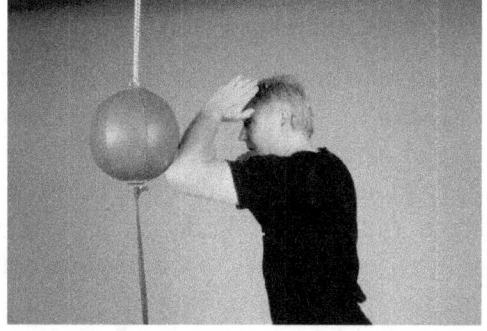

4. Elbow-Elbow – Hit the bag with a rear horizontal elbow, and as the bag returns towards you, hit it with a lead elbow hook.

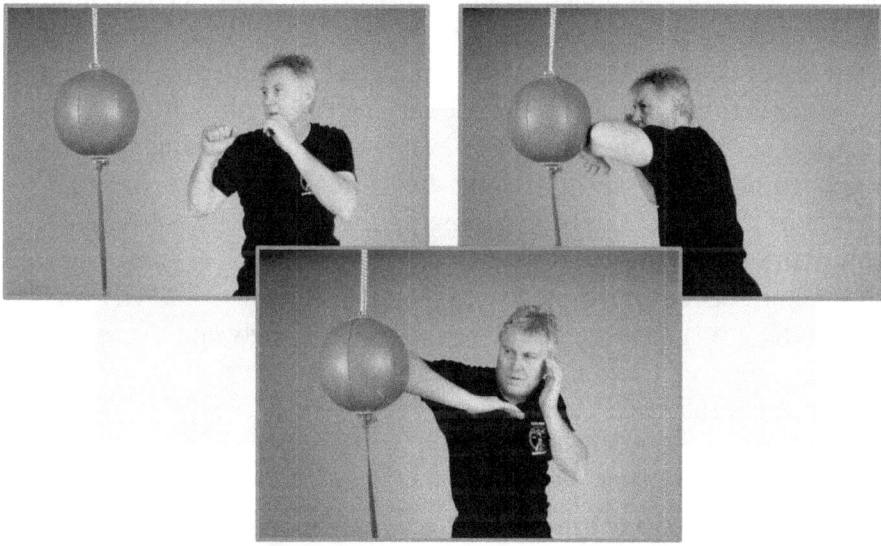

5. Foot-Hand – Hit the bag with a slide-step lead hook kick, then drop forward and as the bag returns, hit it with a lead backfist.

Use of Rhythm and Broken Rhythm

The use of rhythm is an important tactical element in fighting. A martial artist who is able to impose his own rhythm on a fight has a decided advantage of being in control of the situation, and the top-and-bottom bag is a great tool to help you develop an understanding of rhythm, cadence and tempo. While it's impossible to illustrate rhythm or broken rhythm properly in a book, you can at least get an understanding of the principle behind it. When you first begin training with the top-and-bottom bag the idea is to develop a feel for the bag and a sense of rhythm. Start by working on simple actions such as a lead straight punch. Then, as you progress, work compound actions such as a lead straight punch, rear cross, lead horizontal elbow combination. Once you've got a feel for the rhythm of a particular action, you can then start varying the rhythm or use what is known as "broken rhythm." For example, when working a three-punch combination such as "one-two-three", you can vary the rhythm of the combination by changing the speed with which each blow in the combination is thrown (fast – fast – fast, slow – fast - fast, etc.). To use broken rhythm, you first establish a particular rhythm, then break it by inserting a split-second "pause" between two of the motions. One way to do this is to use a metronome set to a specific rhythm, and practice hitting "between the beats."

Training Defensive Actions

You can also use the top-and-bottom bag to help develop your defensive skills. The following examples illustrate various evasion skills that can be practiced on the top-and-bottom bag when it is in motion:

> **a) Push shuffle retreat** – use a push shuffle retreat to evade the bag as it moves towards you.

b) **Slide-step retreat** – use a slide-step retreat to evade the bag as it moves towards you.

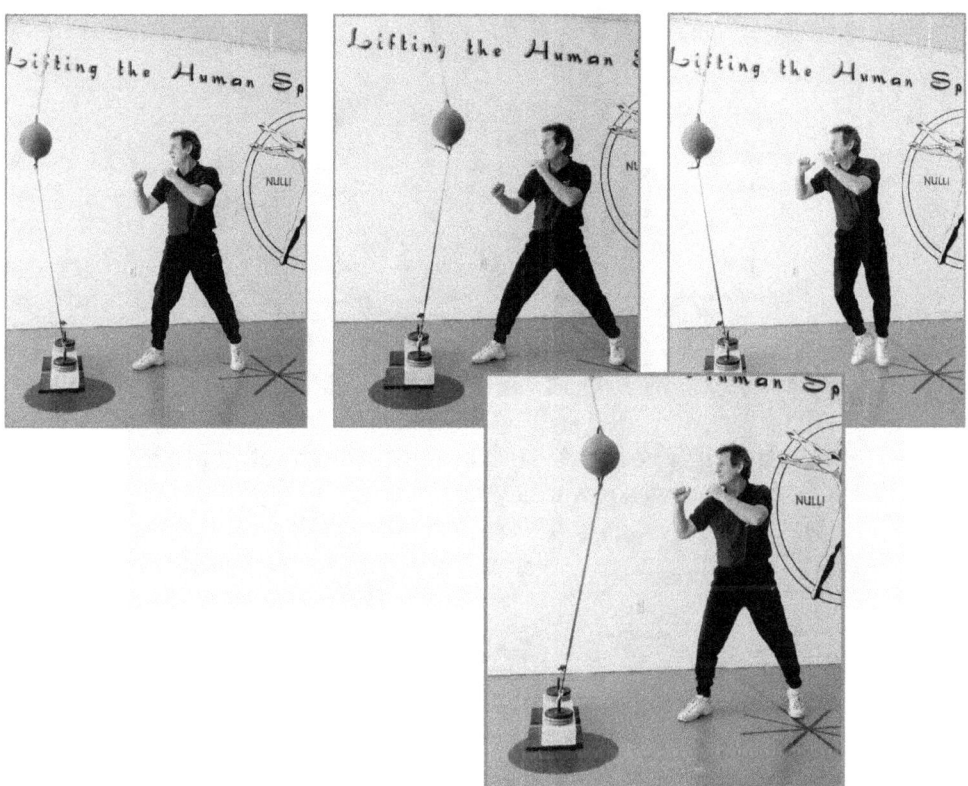

c) **Sidestep right** – use a right sidestep to evade the bag as it moves towards you.

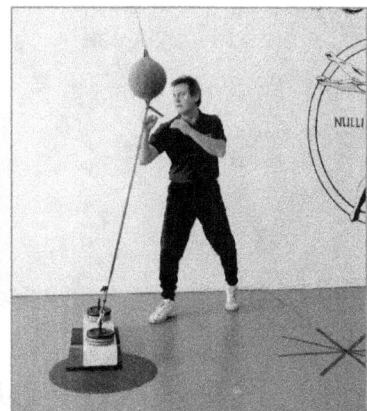

d) **Sidestep left** – use a left sidestep to evade the bag as it moves towards you.

e) **Step-through retreat** – use a step-through retreat to evade the bag as it moves towards you.

f) **Snap away** – use an upper-body "snap-away" to evade the bag as it moves towards you.

DOUBLE END BAG

g) Slip right– slip to the right of the bag as it moves towards you.

h) Slip left – slip to the left of the bag as it moves towards you.

i) Shoulder roll away – use a shoulder roll to move away from the bag as it moves towards you.

NOTE: *Defensive actions such as the duck, bob and weave, etc. can also be used when working on the top and bottom bag but aren't ordinarily trained by themselves.*

Training Aids for the Top-and-Bottom Bag:

1. Keep it "alive" – combine your various strikes on the bag with all types of footwork, body angulations and evasions. Keep yourself well-covered at all times when working on the bag.

2. Concentrate on hitting the bag squarely (by this I mean the correct line or path of force for the particular blow).

3. Work first on developing your sense of rhythm, then move on to varying the rhythm and using "broken-rhythm."

CHAPTER SIX
Wall Bag

The wall bag is a canvas or vinyl bag that hangs on the wall (although it can also be used flat on the ground or a table) and is used to help develop depth and penetration in your blows, as well as giving you a feeling of actually hitting someone. It also helps strengthen your wrist to support your blows. In addition to striking the bag with your hands (punches, slaps, etc.), various elbow techniques and even certain kicking actions can also be applied to it. The bag can be filled with rice, beans, sand, or in some cases even small ball-bearings or stones. (Please Note – I do not recommend using any form of hard filling such as ball-bearings, stones, etc. unless you've spent a great deal of time preparing your hands first and are very knowledgeable about hand conditioning). The following examples illustrate the use of various strikes on the wall bag:

a) Lead straight punch (head level)

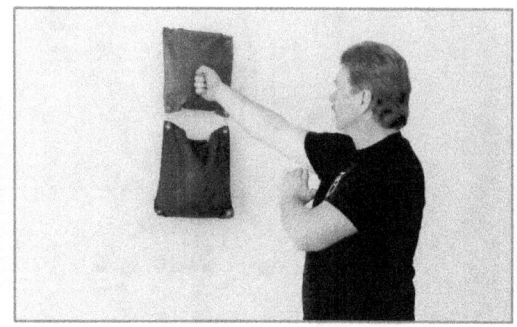

b) Rear straight punch (head level)

c) Lead straight punch (body level)

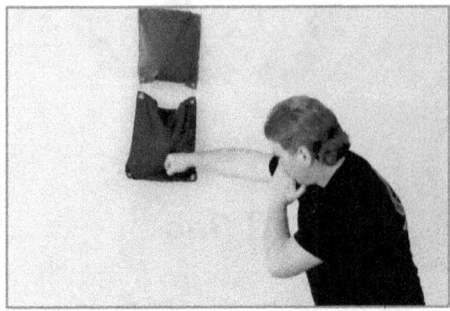

d) Rear straight punch (body level)

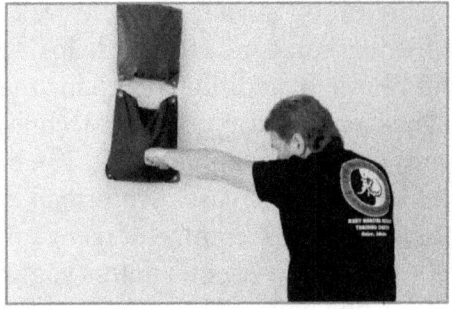

e) Lead hook punch (head level)

f) Rear hook punch (head level)

WALL BAG

g) Lead hook punch (body level)

h) Rear hook punch (body level)

i) Lead straight palm smash

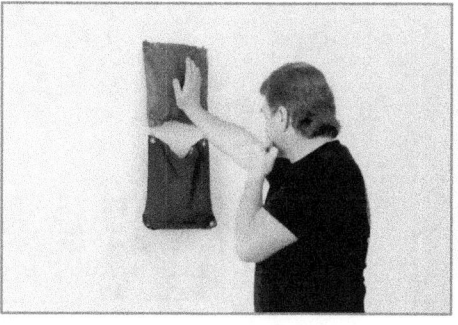

j) Rear straight palm smash

k) Rear overhand palm smash

l) Backfist

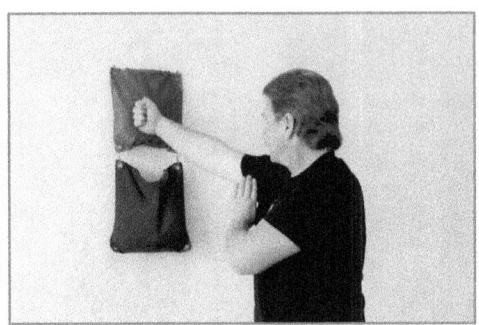

m) Rear horizontal elbow

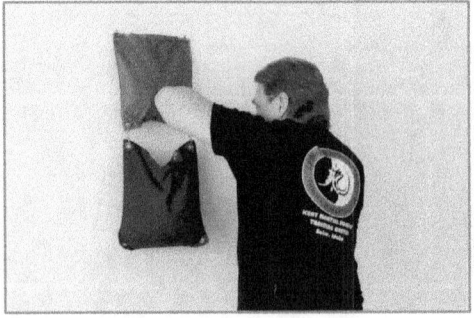

n) Rear diagonal downward elbow

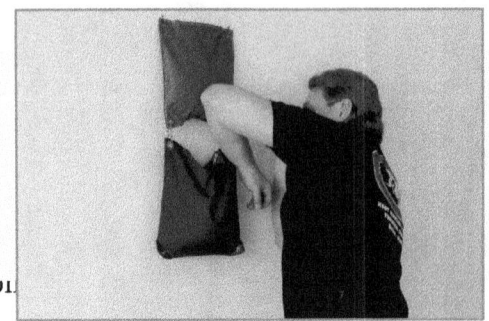

WALL BAG

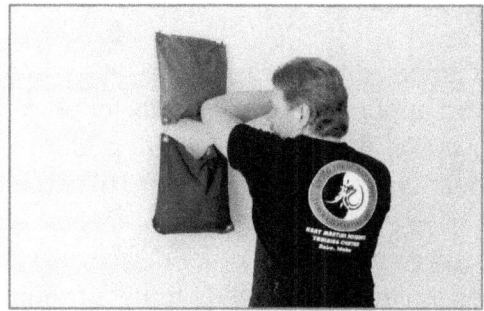

p) Backward elbow

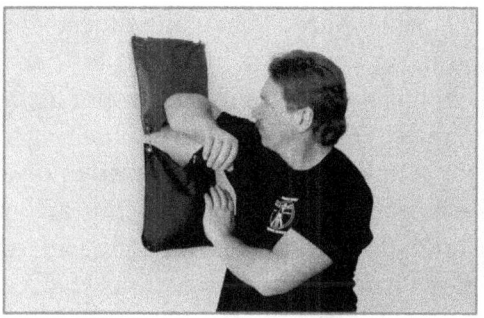

q) Lead hook kick with toe of shoe

Training Tips:

1) Start off easily and lightly when working out on the bag. Remember that conditioning takes time, so make sure to give your hands time to recover between training sessions.

2) If you're working punches, be sure that your wrist is straight and your fist is in proper alignment when your blow lands. Besides working punches, be sure to work slapping actions as well.

3) Have bags set at different heights (head level, body level).

4) Make sure to work the correct body-mechanics of a blow (proper waist torque, etc.) and proper defensive coverage when striking.

Paper Target

The paper target is a useful training tool to help increase your speed and develop correct application of your body for power. An easy piece of equipment to make, it's basically nothing more than a sheet of paper (other materials can be substituted for paper, including plastic sheet protectors or even old medical x-ray sheets) that's hung on a heavy rope or chain, or from some other device, usually around head height. The paper target can also be held by a training partner who can vary the height for you. I've seen more elaborate (and expensive) versions that attach to a heavy bag now starting to appear in martial art magazines. The prime purpose in using the paper target is to help develop waist torque in your punching and hip movement in both side and hook kicking, as well as learning proper distance in striking. It can also help improve your speed. When punching the paper target, the main principle is to keep your arm relaxed and your fist loose as you shoot out the blow as fast and hard as you can, and tighten your fist a split second before it makes contact with the target. The following examples illustrate various actions that can be practiced against the paper target:

a) Lead straight punch

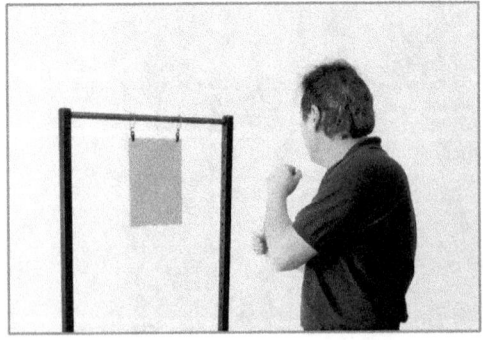 

b) Lead backfist (sideways)

c) Lead hook (sideways)

d) Lead hook kick

e) Lead side kick

Small Plastic/Tennis Ball:

Simply, a small plastic whiffle ball or tennis ball that's suspended from the end of a length of chain by a piece of cord several inches in length. The cord gives the ball flexibility when struck, while the weight of the chain restricts the ball's motion so that it doesn't fly all over the place. The height of the ball can be varied by simply adjusting the length of the chain. Various kicks and strikes can be thrown at the ball as part of shadow boxing to practice balance, control and accuracy in motion.

a) Lead straight punch

b) Rear straight punch

c) Hook punch

d) Hook kick

CHAPTER SEVEN

The Wooden Dummy (Mook Jong)

There are certain specialized pieces of equipment that can be used to develop specific combative skills or qualities. One of these is the Wooden Dummy (Mook Jong) which can be a very effective tool in helping you develop the ability to momentarily immobilize or 'trap' one or both of the opponent's arms during the course of fighting.

As I stated in the Introduction, this book is not about training in any particular style or system. However, it's helpful to understand the principles of one of the forms of attack utilized in Jeet Kune Do which is known as Hand Immobilization Attack in order to utilize the dummy to its full potential in assisting your development as a martial artist.

In a combative situation, regardless of who initiates an attack, when two opponents close the distance and "crash" with each other, the fighters will often find one or both of their arms making contact with the arms of the opponent. Observe how often boxers and mixed martial art fighters end up in some form of clinch or position of touch when they close with each other or are engaged in close-range fighting. This is where Hand Immobilization Attack (HIA) can come into play. The fundamental principle of Hand Immobilization Attack is that you momentarily trap and neutralize either one or both of an opponent's arms while you attack simultaneously with your own strike. Trapping and controlling the opponent's arms allows you to maneuver an them where you want them, and to create a situation whereby the opponent is forced to give you a reaction that will be detrimental to him. They might not want to, but they have no choice or they'll end up getting hit. In addition, by trapping one or both of an opponent's limbs as you close the distance to attack you can limit the possibility of them being able to stop-hit you as you are coming in. Furthermore, trapping or immobilizing and opponent's arm can make it difficult for them to parry by confusing them. Some people consider hand immobilization attack to be a form of grappling as you are grabbing or pinning the opponent's arms. Bruce Lee was renowned for his ability to shut down an opponent's ability to strike and totally immobilize their arms using his highly-developed, lightning-fast trapping skills. According to Dan Inosanto, when Lee used trapping actions against you it felt like you were "inside a washing machine on full agitation cycle". Imagine being in a situation where your arms and body are being pushed, pulled, and yanked every which way, while at the same time you're being hit with a non-stop barrage of punches, slaps, kicks, knee and elbow strikes, as well as leg sweeps and you'll get the picture. The primary piece of equipment Lee used to help develop his incredible trapping abilities was the Wooden Dummy.

While the wooden dummy will never replace a live training partner, and cannot give you the exact energy that a real opponent might, it's nevertheless a very useful tool for developing power and speed in your trapping techniques, as well as conditioning your forearms and developing your gripping abilities. All of the various hand immobilization techniques a person might use such as *pak sao* (slapping hand), *lop sao* (pulling hand), and *jut sao* (jerking hand) can be practiced full force against the dummy, since unlike a real person, it doesn't feel any pain and can't be damaged. Imagine trying to find a training partner willing to let you work a 'neck whip-lashing' hand trapping action not only at full speed and power, but also over and over for hundreds of repetitions at a time. In addition to helping you develop your immobilization actions, the wooden dummy also teaches you to punch straight, and the extended leg can be used for practicing shin/knee kicks. As with the heavy bag, the wooden dummy is an excellent training tool that you can use without the aid of a training partner.

The normal wooden dummy is a cylindrical wooden post approximately six feet in length with three arms and one leg set at specific angles designed to simulate a human form. This post is suspended by two horizontal cross-beams which pass through it and are anchored to either two vertical upright posts against a wall or a free-standing frame. The dummy is designed in such a way that the top and bottom of the post has a certain degree of both forward and backward and side to side movement. This movement makes its flexible and allows it to absorb shock and rebound when struck correctly. The arms and leg (which are removable) are not rigidly fixed in place but have a certain degree of movement when struck or trapped to simulate the reaction of a real opponent's arms and to offer a more realistic feel.

Lee's wooden dummy had several differences to the conventional dummy. It was erected on a 8' x 8' wood-covered, steel-based platform. The dummy's body, instead of being supported by two wooden slats, was supported by metal leaf springs from an automobile, which allowed the dummy to withstand the force with which Lee worked on it (he kept breaking the wooden slats). The dummy body also had a neck carved in it for grabbing and pulling. The two removable upper arms could be switched to convert them into either a left or right lead hand position. The lower leg was constructed of steel because Bruce kept breaking the wooden ones when practicing shin kicks. In addition, the dummy also had two additional legs placed one on either side of the body.

Training on the wooden dummy can not only dramatically enhance your hand-trapping skills, but also help you:

- Train various parries, blocks, hand strikes, kicks, elbow and knee strikes, sweeps and other leg maneuvers.

- Direct your power properly by learning how to "cut the opponent's tool" and bridge the gap with forward energy

- Maintain a correct angle of your body in relation to the centerline for attacking and defending.

- Develop your mobility while moving around the dummy using various types of footwork in conjunction with hand techniques.

- Learn to flow directly from one movement to another without any interruption of power, momentum and speed.

- Develop instinctive reflex memory to trap by sense of touch as opposed to simply looking.

- Strengthen and condition your forearms, hands, and elbows.

A Modern, Fluid Approach to Wooden Dummy Training

The approach to wooden dummy training discussed in this book differs from traditional training methods in numerous ways. Adapting a more fluid, non-classical, modern boxing-style approach, the trainer works out on the dummy in the same manner they work out on a heavy bag, using their imagination and working on angles, leverage, and precision of motions. Working either in a right or left lead fighting stance, the trainer freelances on the dummy and utilizes not only hand immobilization actions, but also other various offensive, counter-offensive and defensive motions which they use in fighting. The objective is not to learn set patterns, but rather to develop the ability to express yourself combatively on the wooden dummy. If a person chooses to learn classical or traditional sets on the dummy, that's fine. But, unless you are learning a particular style such as Wing Chun gung fu, it's not necessary for you to spend a great deal of time learning them in order for you to utilize the dummy as a training tool.

NOTE: *In most of the following examples, the person training on the dummy will be working out of a right lead position. Simply reverse the actions for a left lead position. Also, for simplicity sake, when facing the dummy, the arm to the left of centerline will be referred to as the 'lead' or 'right' arm, and the arm to the right of the centerline will be referred to as the 'rear' or 'left' arm.*

Facing the Dummy

The following photographs illustrate facing the dummy in a right lead ready position.

Facing left side of dummy in right lead ready position.

Facing centerline of dummy in right lead ready position.

Facing right side of dummy in right lead ready position.

Moving around the Dummy

It's important that you're able to move around the dummy smoothly and easily. While there are different kinds of footwork you can use, the following photographs illustrate how you can transition from one side of the dummy to another (While broken down for clarity, any transition action is actually done in a fluid and smooth single movement. Also, note the defensive coverage of the arms while shifting leads)

Illustrates moving from one side of the dummy to the other in a right lead.

Illustrates moving from one side of the dummy to the other in a left lead.

Conditioning the Forearms

Although it's always more desirable to deflect a strike rather than taking the full force of the blow on your forearms, it's sometimes unavoidable in a rapid exchange. For this reason, a certain amount of forearm conditioning is a necessary ingredient in wooden dummy training. Toughening or conditioning your arms doesn't have anything to do with deforming your hands or continually bruising the bones in your arms. Any form of conditioning should be approached gradually and progressively. The dummy has no ego and feels no pain, so if you train incorrectly the only one that might get hurt is you.

Start off by lightly tapping the dummy and go from there.

The following examples illustrate how to train some of the various basic offensive striking actions while at the same time strengthening and conditioning your forearms. For simplicity sake the trainer is shown in a right lead. Reverse the action for a left lead.

A) Bridging on the Inside with Finger Jab

Facing the dummy in a fighting stance, shoot your finger jab straight along the dummy's centerline, bridging into the inside of the wooden arm with your outside wrist/ forearm area. (Be sure to avoid hitting where your wrist bones join the forearm bones as this can be very painful)

THE WOODEN DUMMY

Illustrates bridging into the dummy arm in ready position using your right hand.

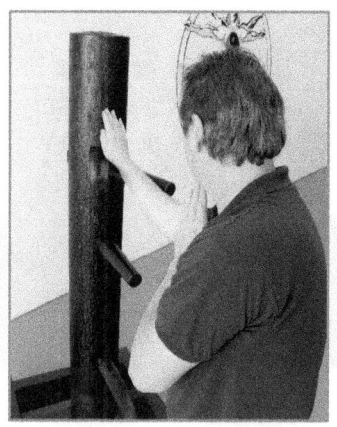

Illustrates bridging into the dummy arm in ready position using your left hand.

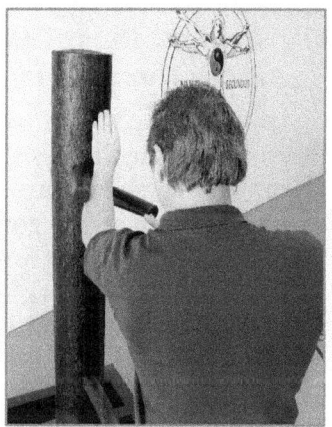

B) Bridging on the Outside with Finger Jab

In this exercise, you bridge across the outer area of the dummy's arms with your finger jab, hitting the wooden arm the inner area of your forearm. Be sure to keep your elbow tucked in and combine your hitting action with a waist twist and slight body angulation.

Illustrates bridging into the outside of the dummy's arm in a ready position with your right hand.

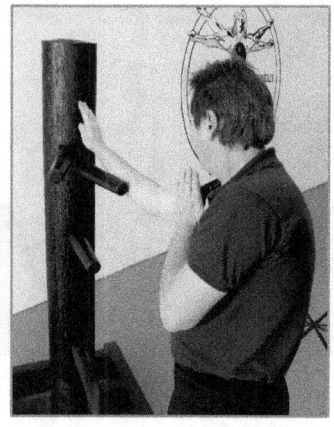

Illustrates bridging into the outside of the dummy's arm in a ready position with your left hand.

C) "Straight Blast" Punching Exercise Moving Across Dummy Arms

In this exercise you work your "straight blast" series of punches while moving across the dummy's upper arms from left to right or vice versa, hitting on both the inside and outside of each wooden arm as you go. This allows you to hit with both the inside and outside of your forearms in rapid succession. It is important to combine footwork with this sequence in order to move from one side of the dummy to the other while you are striking.

D) "Lop Sao" Pulling Hand Exercise Moving Across Dummy Arms

In this exercise you practice a lop sao (grabbing hand) pulling action while moving across the dummy's upper arms from left to right or vice versa, pulling on both the inside and outside of each arm as you go. As with the previous drill, it's important to combine your striking actions with footwork to move from one side of the dummy to the other.

E) "Huen Sao" Wrist Circling Exercise

This exercise is designed to help increase the flexibility and dexterity in your wrists by maintaining contact with the dummy's arms as you move your hands in complete circles around them. The circling action can move in either a clockwise or counter-clockwise direction and can travel either over or under the opponent's. You can work one hand at a time or both hands simultaneously.

These photographs illustrate working the circling action with your left hand, starting from an outside arm position, and finishing in the same position. You could also work on moving from the outside arm position to an inside arm position.

Defensive Actions

The following examples illustrate various defensive parries and deflections that should be trained on the wooden dummy:

1. **Lateral Parry** – a deflecting action which travels on a horizontal line from either left to right or from right to left. Also referred to as a "cross parry", it can be done using either the open palm or the outer/inner area of your wrist.

Illustrates a cross parry from inside to outside using the left hand.

2. **Semicircular Parry** – a deflecting action which travels in a curving arc and can move from high line to low line or from low line to high line. Also referred to sometimes as a "scooping parry", it can be done using either the hand or the outer wrist area of your hand.

Illustrates a semicircular parry traveling from the high line to the low line using the left hand.

3. **Sweeping Parry** – a parry which sweeps into the attacking line and deflects it clear.

Illustrates a sweeping parry traveling from right to left using the right hand. *(See photos on following page.)*

4. **"Fook Sao" Forearm Deflection** – a bent-arm-elbow-in deflecting action using your forearm.

Illustrates a bent arm forearm deflection using the right arm.

5. **"Boang Sao" Deflection** – a raised-elbow deflection which can be used at the high line or the low line position.

Illustrates a raised elbow deflection using the left arm.

Single Immobilization Actions

There are primarily 3 types of immobilizing actions or "traps": (a) slapping or pushing; (b) grabbing or pulling; and (c) hitting, whereby the hit itself acts as an immobilization. The following examples illustrate basic immobilization actions that trap either one or both of the opponent's arms. For convenience sake in the following photographs we will consider that the opponent is in a right lead. Also, be aware that in some of the examples the angles of the hand positions may have been adjusted or exaggerated slightly in order to better illustrate the actions.

1) "Pak Sao" (Slapping Hand)

Pak sao is a slapping trap that can be done with either the lead hand or rear hand, and can be done from various positions, including:

a) Pak sao outside of opponent's lead arm with rear hand and punch on outside of lead arm.

b) Pak sao inside of opponent's lead arm with rear hand and punch on inside of lead arm.

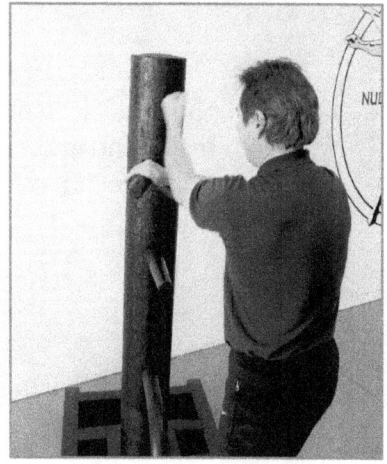

c) Pak sao inside of opponent's rear arm (trapping lead arm also) with rear hand and punch on inside of rear arm.

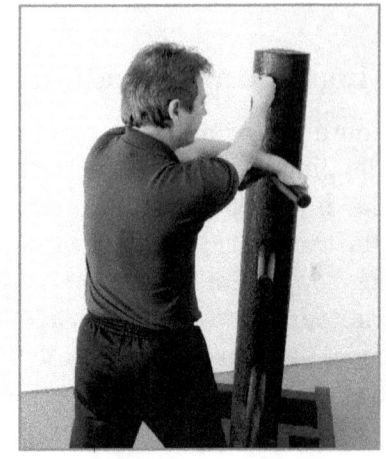

d) Pak sao outside of opponent's rear arm with lead hand and punch with rear hand on outside of rear arm.

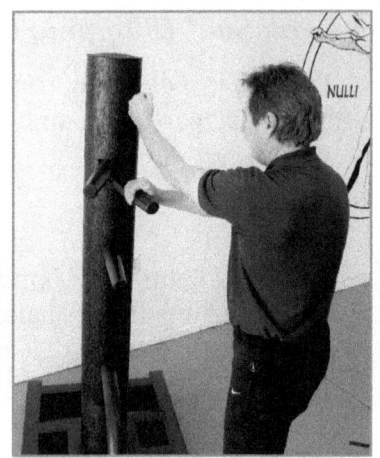

2) "Lop Sao" (Grabbing Hand)

Lop sao is a grabbing or pulling immobilizing action that can be done with either the lead or rear hand, and be done from various positions, including:

a) Lop sao opponent's lead arm with your lead hand and hit with your rear hand on outside.

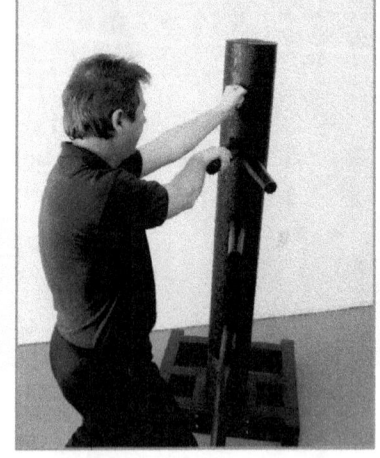

b) Lop sao opponent's rear arm with your rear hand and hit with your lead hand on outside.

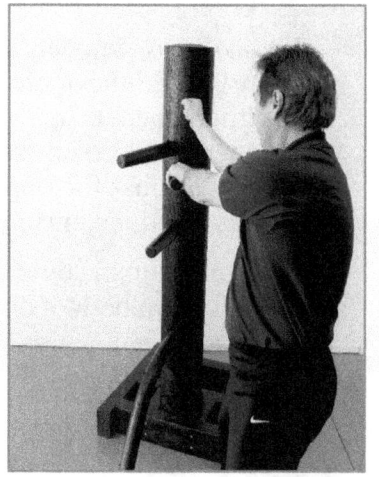

c) Lop sao opponent's rear arm with your lead hand and hit with your rear hand on inside.

d) Lop sao opponent's lead arm with your rear arm from inside position and hit with your lead hand on inside.

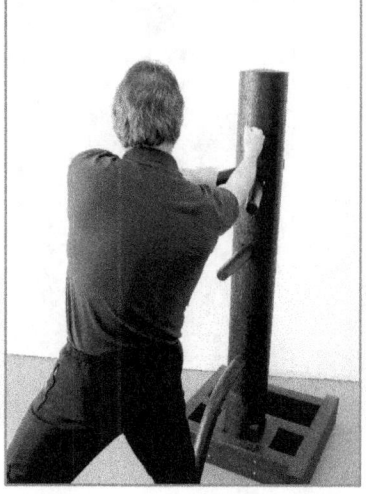

3) *"Jut Sao" (Jerking or Snapping Hand)*

Jut sao is a compact, sudden jerking or snapping action used against either one or both of the opponent's arms that can be used to either open a line of attack or draw a reaction from the opponent that can be used against them. The same action can also be used against the opponent's neck. Jut sao can be done from various positions, including:

a) From a double outside position, use a two-handed jut sao to pull down both of opponent's arms and hit with rear hand.

b) From a double outside hand position, use a rear hand jut sao and hit with your lead hand.

c) From a lead-hand-inside/rear-hand-outside position, jut sao with your rear hand and hit with your lead hand.

d) From a rear-hand-inside/lead-hand-outside position, jut sao with your lead hand and hit with your rear hand.

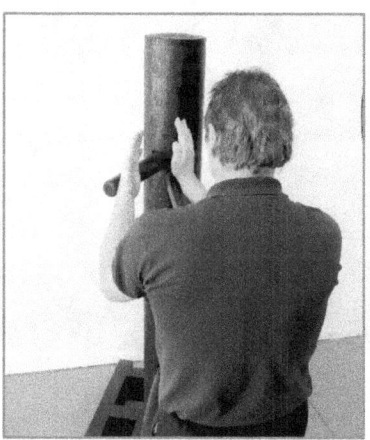 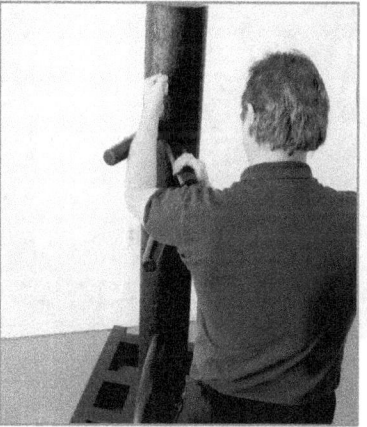

4) "Huen Sao" (Circling Hand)

Huen sao is a circling action using the wrist that travels either over or under the opponent's arm. Unlike the Jao Sao (running hand), the circling hand action usually maintains contact with the opponent's arm and can be used to move your hand either from outside position to an inside position or vice versa. Huen Sao can also be a sharp sudden action that "snaps" the opponent's hand out of position. The following examples illustrate how huen sao can be practiced on the dummy:

a) Using the huen sao to circle over the dummy arm and move from outside to inside position.

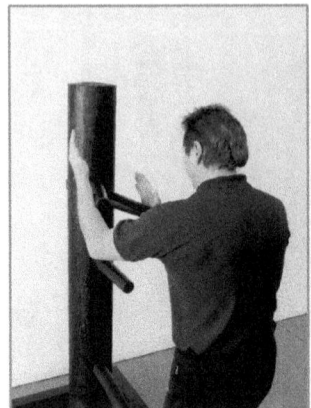  

b) Use the huen sao to circle under the dummy arm and move from inside to outside position.

 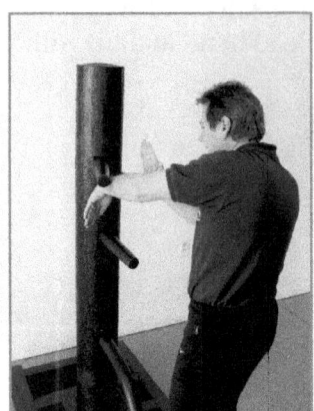 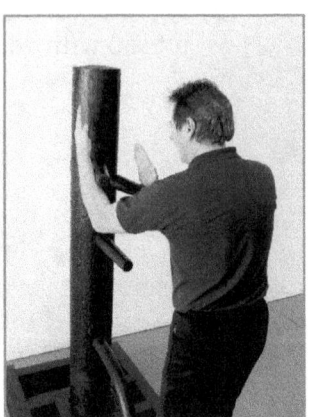

5) *"Jao Sao" (Running Hand)*

While not actually a trapping action, jao sao is used in many hand immobilization actions. It is an action that can you can use to maneuver your hand from one line to another; shifting it from an outside position to an inside position, inside to outside position, outside position to outside position, or from a low position to a high position and vice versa by means of disengagement. The following examples illustrate how jao sao can be practiced on the dummy:

a) **Outside to Outside** – from a high outside position against the dummy's left arm, disengage your lead hand and move it to an outside position against the dummy's right arm.

b) **Outside to Inside** – from a high outside position against the dummy's left arm, disengage your lead hand and move it to an inside position against the dummy's right arm.

c) **High to Low** – from a high outside position against the dummy's right arm, disengage your lead hand and move it to a low position against the lower arm.

d) **Low to High** –from a low outside position against the lower dummy arm, disengage your lead hand and move it to a high outside position against the upper right arm.

Compound Trapping Actions

The following examples illustrate how various trapping actions can be combined when training on the dummy and include forms of attack known as Attack By Combination and Progressive Indirect Attack. In reality, each of the actions in any combination is dependent upon the type of energy you receive against your arms from the opponent *(See section on "Tactile Awareness" in training at end of chapter)*

1) Pak sao with lead straight punch, follow with lead hand lop sao and rear straight punch, inside pak sao with rear hand and lead hand straight punch.

2) Pak sao, lead hand jao sao, double-hand jut sao, inside pak sao with lead straight punch.

3) Pak sao with lead straight punch, rear hand lop sao with lead backfist.

4) Pak sao with lead straight punch, follow with lead hand lop sao with rear straight punch, disengage with lead hand jao sao to groin smash. *(See photos on next page.)*

5) Pak sao with lead straight punch, switch to low lead straight punch, follow with pak sao and backfist.

6) Lead lop sao with rear straight punch, follow with cross parry and low punch, switch to high jao sao with lead hand, finish with right-hand jut sao and left straight punch.

7) Jao sao with lead hand, followed by pak sao with lead hand and rear straight punch punch, finish with lead knee to groin.

8) Use a lead hand jao sao to close the distance and end up with lead hand in high outside position against the opponent's rear arm and rear hand against inside of opponent's lead arm; shift to a lead hand huen sao with left straight punch, followed by inside pak sao and lead straight punch, finish with a lead hand lop sao and rear straight punch.

Bridging the Distance into Trapping

One of the primary objectives in trapping is to gain an attachment against either one or both of the opponent's arms in order to trap them. In order to make your training as realistic as possible, you should practice shifting from punching into trapping, and bridging into trapping from kicking range. The following examples illustrate ways that you can practice shifting into trapping by closing the distance with either a punch or kick:

1) Use a high lead backfist to bridge the distance and gain an attachment against the dummy's right arm. Follow with a lead hand lop sao and rear straight punch. *(See photos on next page.)*

THE WOODEN DUMMY

2) Hit with a high lead finger jab as you close the distance and gain an attachment against the inside of opponent's right arm, follow with a rear hand pak sao as you disengage the lead hand to hit with a high backfist.

3) Hit with a low lead straight punch as you close the distance and gain an attachment against the right side of the dummy's lower arm, follow with a rear hand pak sao as you disengage and hit with a high backfist.

4) Hit with a high lead straight punch as you close the distance and gain an attachment against the inside of the dummy's rear arm, finish with a lead hand lop sao and rear hand straight punch on outside of dummy's lead arm.

5) Feint a low lead straight punch and shift to a high lead palm hook to close the distance and gain an attachment against the outside of both of the dummy's arms, follow with two-hand jut sao, finish with a straight blast of punches.

6) Feint a high palm hook as you close the distance, then fire a rear straight punch to gain an attachment against the outside of dummy's lead arm, finish with a rear hand jut sao with lead hand straight punch.

7) Feint a low lead straight punch which shifts to a high lead straight punch inside the opponent's rear guard as you close the distance and gain an attachment against both the opponent's arms (one inside-one outside); follow with a lead hand lop sao and rear hand straight punch across outside of dummy's lead arm, finish with a rear hand cross cross-parry and lead hand palm smash to groin.

8) Feint a lead finger jab as you close the distance, followed by a rear finger jab to gain an attachment against the inside of the opponent's lead arm, finish with a rear hand lop sao and lead straight punch.

9) Use a low lead side kick to close the gap from kicking range, followed by a high lead finger jab to gain an attachment against the inside of the opponent's rear arm, finish with a lead hand lop sao and rear straight punch.

10) Use a lead-leg foot obstruction kick to close the gap from kicking range, pak sao the dummy's lead arm as you recover forward and hit with a lead straight punch.

11) Feint a low lead hook kick followed by a low lead straight punch feint to close the distance, follow with a high jao sao to gain an attachment against the outside of both of the dummy's arms, finish with double jut sao and knee to the groin.

Other Methods of Using the Wooden Dummy

As I stated at the beginning of this chapter, we are not approaching wooden dummy training from the perspective of a particular martial art style or system. In addition to using the wooden dummy to develop and improve your trapping skills, you can also use it to develop economical motions and condition your forearms for boxing-style actions. Again, start out easy – don't try to "kill" the dummy.

The following examples illustrate how you can work your boxing style punches on the dummy:

a) Fire a lead rear straight punch into the dummy's centerline, then hit into the dummy's upper arm with a lead hook.

b) Feint a low lead straight punch as you slip to the right, then hit into the dummy's upper arm with a high rear hook.

c) Fire a low lead uppercut into the dummy's lower arm, then shift to a high rear hook into the dummy's upper arms.

d) Slip to the left to avoid a punch at your head, then fire a low rear uppercut into the dummy's lower arm, followed by a high lead hook into the upper arms.

e) Crash to double outside hand position, double jut sao, then use an elbow pop-up and simulate a shoot to grappling position. (You need to remove the lower dummy arm and leg in order to do this. Also, do not slam your shoulder into the dummy, just work body positioning).

The Use of "Tactile Awareness" in Hand Immobilization Attack

A major element in the successful use of hand immobilization attack is a high level of "tactile awareness" which enables you to feel the various types of energies an opponent's arms exert against your own when you make contact with them. For example, is the opponent's energy hard, soft, inward, outward, upward, downward, or straight forward? Tactile awareness is important because the type of energy the opponent gives can be a deciding factor in what action or actions you use against them. As the wooden dummy cannot give you these various energies, it will be necessary for you to use your imagination in training to simulate them. (You will only be able to do this if you've practiced with a real training partner feeding the various energies to you). You can refer to ***"The Encyclopedia of JKD"*** for descriptions and illustrations of these various energies.

Training Tips for working with the Wooden Dummy:

1) Start slowly and gradually increase the force with which you work on the dummy in order to avoid possibly injuring your hands or arms.

2) Make sure you are working the correct angle of your body in relation the dummy when working your offensive and defensive actions. Direct your power properly by "cutting into the opponent's tool" and bridging the gap with forward energy

3) Move around the dummy using light, smooth footwork in conjunction with your hand techniques. Flow smoothly from one movement to the next.

4) "Listen" with your arms and feel how the dummy reacts to your various actions.

5) Proper height of the dummy is important for correct usage. However, at times it's good to work against dummies of various heights so that you can adapt your actions to opponents of different heights.

6) Constantly experiment to find new ways of using the dummy in your training.

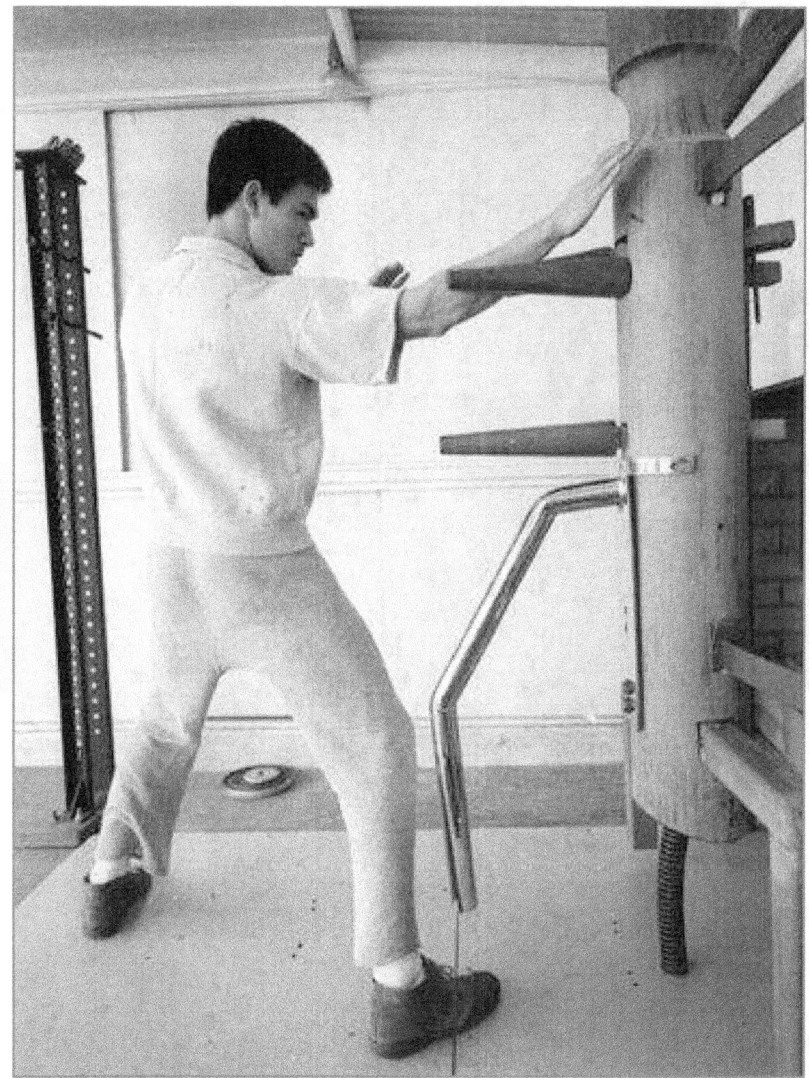

Conclusion

There are numerous approaches to working out on the wooden dummy. The method or methods you choose to use and how much time you spend practicing on it is an individual thing. You can hit it hard if you're used to it and want to work on conditioning your forearms. If you're training on it late at night and don't want to disturb the neighbors or the rest of your family, you can work on it very lightly and focus on proper positioning. As with the heavy bag, the dummy has no ego and it feels no pain. So, remember, if you train incorrectly on it the only person who will end up getting hurt is you.

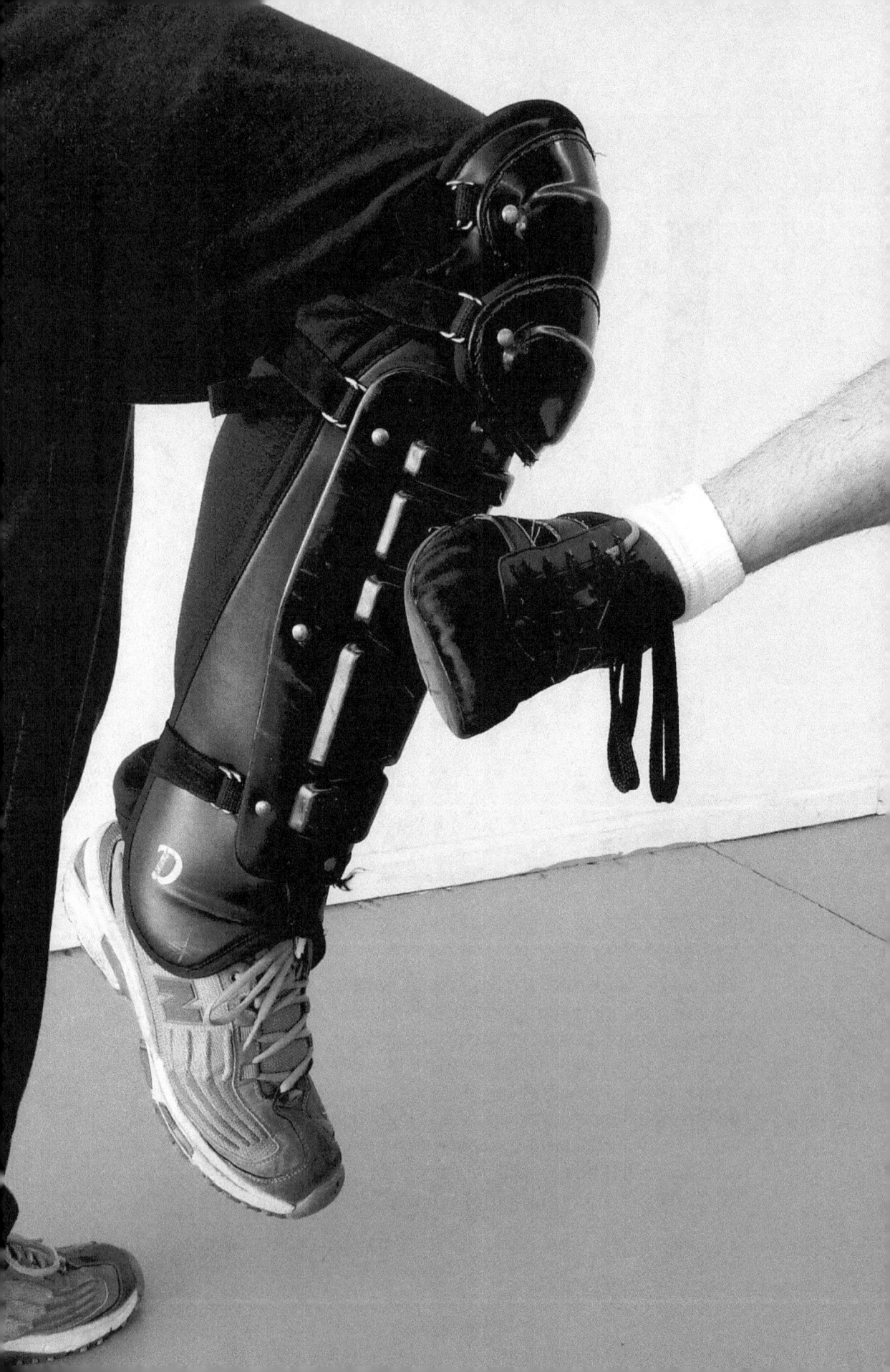

CHAPTER EIGHT

Training with Protective Body Equipment

Besides training with equipment such as focus gloves, heavy bag, kicking shield, etc., you can also utilize many of the same training principles and methods with protective body equipment such as boxing gloves, chest protectors, shinguards, etc. Or you can use a combination of both protective body equipment and training equipment.

In this photograph *(at left)* the trainer wears a chest protector, hard shin guard, and holds a set of Thai forearm pads.

In this photograph *(at right)* the trainer wears a chest protector, hard shin guard, and holds a set of focus gloves.

These photographs illustrate the training partner working an offensive combination against the trainer who is wearing protective body equipment and focus gloves. The partner attacks with a low side kick, followed by a lead straight, rear straight, hook punching combination, followed by a neck clinch tie up and knee to the stomach.

As with the numerous types of training equipment, there are a variety of different types of protective body equipment available on the market today. What type you choose will depend to a great extent on the type of training you intend to engage in and what you wear while training. For example, there are soft, flexible shinguards and hard, solid shinguards, each of which is utilized for a different purpose. If the person I'm training is wearing tennis shoes and intends to practice hard kicks to my shins over and over, I will wear a solid shinguard in order to protect my shin from the constant and sustained pounding it will take. On the other hand, if I'm engaged in a light sparring session, I may wear soft shinguards or even none at all.

Hard shinguards will allow your leg to withstand repeated kicks to without injury.

If you are training your partner to deliver hard knee strikes or elbow strikes to the body, it makes sense to wear some form of body protector.

Again, the main point to keep in mind is why you are using the equipment. Do not allow it to become a 'crutch' that will permit you to do things you normally wouldn't do. For example, I've seen people wearing hard shinguards when they're sparring, and using them as 'armor' when they cover or block an opponent's kicks. This gives them a false sense of security because they don't learn how to absorb or dissolve the force correctly, and they end up running into trouble when they're no wearing them and receive a hard kick.

An excellent training method I assimilated during my training with members of the Boxe Francaise-Savate National Team from France is that of placing your boxing gloves on various parts of the body to act as targets for your partner to hit. This develops not only accuracy and precision in striking while moving, but also rapid 'line-recognition' skills. The following photographs illustrate some of the various ways the boxing gloves can be used to set various target lines.

a) Lead hook kick (low line)

b) Lead hook kick (middle line)

TRAINING WITH PROTECTIVE BODY EQUIPMENT

c) Lead hook kick (high line)

d) Rear hook kick (low line)

e) Rear hook kick (middle line)

f) Rear hook kick (high line)

g) Lead side kick (low line)

h) Lead side kick (middle line)

i) Lead side kick (high line)

j) Lead straight punch to the body

k) Lead shovel hook punch to the solar plexus

This training method can be used to develop both single and compound actions and develop your offensive and counter-offensive skills. The following are examples of how you can develop your counter-offensive skills:

In this example, the training partner evades the opponent's rear straight punch to the head by shifting outside and counters with a lead shovel hook to the body.

In this example the training partner evades the opponent's rear straight punch and simultaneously counters with a lead hook kick to the ribs.

Conclusion

As with any other form of training equipment (when working with a partner) the workout you receive will depend to a great extent upon your training partner's knowledge, skill, and creativity as a feeder.

The "tools of the trade" (the body's natural weapons such as hands feet, elbows, knees, etc.) available to the martial artist are universal. How finely your martial art "instrument" is tuned will determine, to a large extent, the degree of efficiency and effectiveness with which you are capable of utilizing these various weapons. Reality is the key to training for any martial artist. And the proper use of training equipment can help you come as close to reality as possible and hone and sharpen your skills and techniques, all of which go a long way in helping you to actualize your full potential. As such, the inclusion of equipment training is a vital ingredient in your overall development as a complete martial artist. Furthermore, by utilizing a variety of training equipment you will not only stimulate your interest and challenge your coordination but help ward off motivational boredom and physical or mental stagnation in your training.

Each piece of training equipment you use should serve a specific purpose and offer an exciting challenge to you as you're mastering your skills. There's nothing secret or special about training equipment. Uniqueness is a product of creativity. Training equipment also doesn't have to be elaborate or expensive to be effective. While it might be great to be able to afford to buy the best equipment available, some people might not have that option. However, improvisation coupled with imagination can create all types of work out equipment. I've seen a double-end bag created out of an inflated plastic ball you buy for a couple of dollars and an old pair of panty hose. Necessity, as they say, is the mother of invention. However, regardless of whether the equipment you use is store-bought or homemade, it should be durable and able to withstand you kicks, punches and other strikes without breaking or falling apart. It should also give you an appropriate "feeling" when you hit it, so you understand what it feels like to really land a blow against an opponent.

Remember that the effectiveness of training equipment rests in the way it's used, and that any type of equipment is only as good as the person using it, or the trainer feeding it. So whether you're working out with a partner or by yourself, imagine that the equipment is a "live" opponent that is moving and fighting, and maintain your "combative awareness." Train with the proper mental attitude and invest all of your actions with "emotional content" (physical and mental intensity and energy). Develop "body-feel" in all your actions. For example, when you're hitting a focus mitt, how does your hand feel when your blow lands? How does the focus glove feel against your hand? What kind of sound does it make? What happens to the feeder's arm? Does it fly away or barely move? This complete focus of attention to what you are doing is what is referred to as "immersion in the moment". If you do this when you practice, even basic routines like heavy bag work can become a palette for your own self-expression.

Finally, keep in mind that training with equipment is a means to an end and not the end itself. Recognize that any type of equipment has limitations, and that overuse of any particular piece of equipment can have a negative affect on the transfer of skill. And remember that regardless of what type of training equipment you use, to achieve the results you want, it's necessary to put forth the time and effort necessary to develop and maintain a consistent training regimen that's geared to improving some aspect of your physical development on a daily basis.

Good Luck, Good Training, and KEEP BLASTING!

Appendix A

"Achieving Personal Martial Art Excellence"

The ultimate objective for any martial artist is to have the ability to "fit in" with any type of opponent and express themselves without restrictions or confinement in combat. To accomplish this you need to have the ability to move your body and adapt to whatever type of opponent you happen to be facing, and relate your various punches, kicks, strikes, locks, throws, etc. as part of an intuitive arsenal from any angle and at any given moment. How is it possible to achieve such a level of self-mastery? The answer lies in under-standing and utilizing what is referred to as "the Training Process"; a systematic and progressive approach to training that will take you from whatever level you are currently at as a martial artist, to where you ultimately want to be.

Understanding the Training Process

The training process serves a very clear and definite purpose, which is to develop and prepare you for the highest levels of performance in all of the various combative elements such as kicking, striking, trapping, grappling, etc. All of these various combative elements are interrelated and should be viewed, not as separate entities, but rather as links of a chain that are interconnected together. Each of the individual links, while an integral part of the chain, is but a single part of a unified 'whole'. None of the links is any more or less important than any of the others. A lack of understanding as to how the various combative elements are interconnected will make it difficult for you to understand the essence of the training process and master the methods of its structuring and planning.

APPENDIX A

Elements of the Training Process

The Training Process is comprised of all the learning methods and elements, including self-teaching, that are aimed at improving your overall abilities. Armed with the understanding that the better the process used, the better the results that should be achieved, it makes sense that you should organize your own training process with a lot of foresight. Regardless of your training level, there are certain fundamental or "core" elements that should be included in your training process. These elements include:

1) Physical Conditioning – As I stated earlier, your body is the "instrument" you use in martial arts. It's the engine and delivery system for all of your techniques, actions, etc. The physical conditioning element of training concentrates on building the essential prerequisites for high efficiency, and this includes such things as the development of strength, power, flexibility, and endurance in order to cultivate a condition of total health and fitness. There are various approaches to each of these aspects of conditioning and you should research and experiment to discover which ones work best for you. Refuse to limit yourself to only one training method or way of working out.

2) Technique and Coordination Training – Good technique and a high level of neuromuscular coordination will enable you to make economical and optimum use of your physical condition. Technique training means not only the development of technical skills, but also the stabilization those learned skills so that you can use them with consistency under all kinds of conditions. Physical Conditioning and Technique training should always go hand in hand, because as you develop your strength, stamina, speed, power, etc., you should keep improving the quality and standard of your technique.

3) Tactical/Strategic Training – Strategy is often described as the overall plan of action a fighter intends to use to win a fight, whereas tactics are the actions used moment by moment during the fight to carry out that strategy. Development of both your tactical and strategic capacities enable you to make optimum use of your physical condition and technical skills in conjunction with your psychological capacity in responding effectively to an opponent's strengths and weaknesses, reading their "playbook" or "game-plan", and in being able to adapt or "fit in" to any situation.

Both technique/coordination training and tactical/strategic training combine to comprise a large part of any martial artist's overall training process, and as I said before, are interconnected. The cultivation of these elements can be broken down into three phases or stages:

Stage 1 – Synchronization of "Self" – The acquisition of skill is a primary consideration in the basic development of any martial artist. In other words, you have to develop and know how to use your tools. Every combative skill has its own technique, its own motion that needs to be developed and perfected. You have to learn a technique first, the same way you learn any lesson, through consistent practice and repetition ("alive" repetition, not non-thinking, "robotic" repetition). At this stage of training the focus is primarily on acquiring technical skills and becoming consistent in their performance. During this stage of training you work on synthesizing various weapons or techniques into your arsenal and synchronizing the actions or skills into your body by developing such qualities as:

- **a) Correct Form** -- This means the most efficient manner in which you can use a motion, and includes such things as proper body mechanics, non-telegraphic initiation, proper understanding and use of leverage, good balance (both stationary and in movement), economical use of motion and energy, proper follow-through, and good defensive coverage.

- **b) Precision** –This refers to accuracy and the ability to place your weapon on the desired target. Precision could also relate to using proper leverage when you are applying a joint lock or installing a choke on an opponent.

- **c) Rhythm** – In this regard, rhythm refers to developing your ability to combine various simple/single movements into compound/combination actions (such as a lead hook kick, lead straight punch, rear elbow strike combination), and link them together so that they flow naturally and with a sense of rhythm.

At the same time, you're developing the above qualities, the speed at which a technique or action you're practicing should be progressively increased. This is what we mean by "<u>synchronization of the whole</u>." The idea is to take any technique or action, develop the proper body-mechanics and ultimately "make it your own." Stage 1 is of paramount importance in your overall training process because it sets the foundations for all future work, and inadequate or poor preparation at this stage will inevitably lead to problems down the road in your training.

APPENDIX A

Stage 2 – Synchronization with the Opponent – This phase of training deals with transforming the performance factors that you've developed into new higher and more complex standards of performance. At this stage, the primary emphasis is on refining the skills and coordination you developed in Stage 1 and developing your proficiency in using them in varying circumstances. The techniques or actions you've learned are now practiced under more combat-like conditions in which you have to regulate your speed, distance, and rhythm, etc. in order to relate to or "synchronize" with the opponent you're up against. In Stage 2 you also work on developing such essential combative qualities as:

- **Timing** – In this case, timing refers to the ability to seize an opportunity when it is either given or created. You may know how to do a technique, and even have adequate speed and distance, but without correct timing it is less than likely that action will be successful.

- **Distance** – Distance refers to maintaining the spatial relationship between yourself and an opponent in order to attack or counterattack the moment an opening appears. For example, you may possess the ability to kick fast and hard, but if you lack the ability to regulate or control distance, it's more than likely your kick may not land.

Stage 3 -- Application Under Fighting Conditions -- In this stage of training, conditions approximating various combat conditions are simulated, and you work on applying the techniques and actions you've learned against a 'non-cooperative', contesting opponent who is not only attempting to provoke errors on your part by blocking or countering with timing and distance, but who is also attempting to hit or counter you . The development of proper combative attitude and your problem-solving abilities are stressed during this stage of training. It is only through combative training such as freelance sparring with all types of opponent's (tall, short, fast, powerful, uncoordinated, etc.) that you develop your ability to compete to the best advantage against any type of opponent, to expend your strength and energy reserves with maximum economy and sense of purpose and develop the mental qualities specific to fighting.

The final core element of the Training Process is:

4) Mental Training – The achievement of outstanding performance levels depends substantially on the development of a martial artist's mental abilities. It is one thing to possess the physical elements noted above, yet quite another to use them when it counts. Physical consistency usually goes hand in hand with mental or psychological consistency.

Mental training utilizes methods that combine physical preparation with psychological preparation and aid not only in the development of mental faculties such as critical-thinking skill and power of observation and analysis, but also in developing such qualities as self-reliance, concentration, willpower, and perseverance. Mental training also includes the use of such things as relaxation and visualization exercises to help you deal with performance-reducing stumbling blocks such things as anxiety, negative thinking, etc. Finally, mental training includes the development of your ability to creatively apply training knowledge and principles to your own training. As with the physical conditioning component, there are various approaches and numerous training methods you can use for the different aspects of mental training, and you should research and experiment to discover which ones work best for you.

Developing Your Personal Training Process

Training is to a very great extent an individual matter. Each individual is different as far as such things as speed, power, flexibility, coordination, endurance, etc. are concerned. As such, while the main core training elements apply across the board to every martial artist, the training process you use should be designed specifically for yourself. Ultimately, it will be the structure and quality of your training process that will determine how far you tap your full potential as a martial artist. In order for you to actualize your full potential, you should approach your training progressively, and in a scientific manner. While remaining flexible and adaptable, there should be nothing random or haphazard about it. Developing your own training process involves three primary steps:

1) Set Training Goals -- The setting of training goals is an important and integral part of any martial artist's training process. Why? Because a goal is an objective, a target. It's a clear, "This is what I'm working toward," or "This is what I want to achieve." Goals are necessary for direction. If you don't have them, it can become easy for you to drift, stagnate, or follow wrong paths in your training. Lack of training goals can lead to decreased motivation, haphazard training, lack of focus and concentration, and lowered performance potential. On the other hand, well-defined training goals can increase your motivation, concentration and focus, encourage persistence and intensity in training, and lead to improved performance potential. Training goals are also useful for feedback purposes. They provide you with a reference point, and by comparing your current position with the reference point you can figure out what adjustments or corrections you might need to make.

How do you go about setting training goals? The first step is to get a clear fix on where you want to go by asking yourself, "What do I want to accomplish with my training?" Again, this is a very individualized thing. Each person is different with regard to such things as level of physical fitness, flexibility, coordination, technical skill level, etc. So your technical and non-technical supplementary training should be set for your specific needs. While it's okay to be inspired by great martial artists or champion athletes in other athletic endeavors, simply trying to copy or follow their training routines may be detrimental to your own training. For example, it would not be in best interest of a martial artist just beginning their training to attempt to throw over 18,000 punches in a single month as the late Bruce Lee used to do. If they did they would probably end up injuring themselves. It's also important when setting your training goals to be as specific as possible. Vague or poorly defined goals will lead to poor or sporadic results. For example, don't just say, "My goal is to become flexible." Be specific. What type of flexibility do you want, static, dynamic, or both? What specific areas of your body do you want to make more flexible? Your legs? Back? Shoulders? Refine your objective down to something clear-cut such as, "My goal is to be able to achieve a full-split position with my legs." Once you have identified specific training goals, write them down, because a written goal serves as a contract with yourself and tells you that the work has officially begun.

2) Research the best ways to accomplish your goal(s) – Once you've established your training goal(s), you then want to find the most efficient and effective methods to achieve your objective(s). How do you go about doing this? The first thing to do is to research your own experience. Look at what you have been doing in your training up to this point and ascertain what is still functional and working and what is not. If you discover a training method or exercise has outlived its productiveness, discard it. The next step is to draw upon all the resources at your disposal. Avail yourself of the knowledge that exists in books, magazines, DVD's etc. Take advantage of the wealth of martial art and fitness training information (physical and mental) available at your fingertips through the internet and other forms of information technology. If you find something you like or, more important, that is functional for you, incorporate it into your training process.

3) Implement the methods and record your progress – After you've figured out how you're going to achieve your goal and implemented methods to reach it, write down the results for each training session. Keeping detailed, written records of your workouts enables you to use them as an on-going record of your journey and allows you to answer such important questions for yourself such as:

- *Are the methods I'm using working or do I need to change them?*
- *Is what I'm doing today getting me closer to where I want to be tomorrow?*
- *Am I making the daily adjustments necessary in my training?*
- *Am I doing all that is required to get me where I would like to be?*

Avoiding Training Pitfalls

While it would be impossible to avoid every problem or mistake that might pop up during training, there are several major pitfalls you should try to avoid in developing your own training process. These include:

- Taking on goals imposed on you by other people such as parents, friends, coaches, etc. Make sure that the goals you have set are your own or you will undoubtedly encounter problems down the road.

- Vainly repeating someone else's training routines or patterns. Don't do something just because someone else tells you to, or because they do it themselves, or because a magazine tells you that a world-champion does it. Make sure everything you do fits you and your training goals.

- Non-thinking, "robotic" repetition in your training. Be 'mindful' in everything you are doing.

APPENDIX A

Maintaining Motivation

There's a saying in athletics that states, "If you want to win, you've got to prepare yourself to win." If your goal is to become the best martial artist that you are capable of being, then you need to train yourself to become the best. It's not going to happen by accident. Talent alone won't do it. Circumstance or luck won't do it either. Attaining the highest levels of performance requires that you, as a martial artist, meet a number of requirements. You need to master the proper techniques and have the necessary tools and skills at your command. You must subject yourself to long and often arduous training, which at times it can be boring, tiring, painful, and conflict with other attractive or otherwise important pursuits. Both of these things require commitment, dedication and a high degree of motivation. In most cases, since the incentives to train are not extrinsic, it will be up to you to provide them for yourself. The more you can make your training interesting and rewarding, the more you provide yourself with the motivation to train. The following are a few ideas you can use to help maintain your motivation in training:

- Turn the search for the best within yourself into an art form. Be creative and free-thinking in your approach to training.

- Use your training as vehicle to discover who you really are, not only as a martial artist, but more importantly, as a unique, living and creative individual.

- View each workout or training session as a learning experience; an opportunity to take yourself to a new level.

- Constantly push the envelope to find your limitations and smash through the barriers to your own physical performance. Each day explore your body's potential to become stronger, faster, more flexible, more efficient at utilizing oxygen, better coordinated, etc.

- Always remain on the lookout for ways to keep your training, fresh, interesting and fun.

JKD: An Art Caught in an Identity Crisis

By Chris Kent

In January 1975, Karate Illustrated published an article written by my good friend and training partner, Gilbert Johnson, titled *"The Furious Pace of JKD – Where Has it Been? Where is it going?"* The article talked about the identity of JKD both during Bruce Lee's life and the perpetuation of the art following his untimely passing. In the article he posed the following question -- *"If JKD changes with the personalities of each practitioner, will it eventually change altogether?* He also wrote -- *"What JKD becomes in the future will depend on what the JKD people of today make it. Lee taught a handful of people what might be described as the most direct route to their own self-expression in the martial arts. They in turn are using similar methods to teach others."*

In this article I'd like to take it a step further and ask the question: "What Has Happened to JKD?" To be completely honest, in many places in the martial art world, the perception of JKD is not particularly great at this time. In recent years some people have commented that JKD has become or is becoming 'irrelevant' in today's martial art world. Others have stated that the art is obsolete. While I disagree with both of these perspectives, it's clear to see that over the years JKD's image has become tarnished, and upon close inspection it's not difficult to see why – Jeet Kune Do is an art caught in an identity crisis.

Numerous misperceptions and distortions regarding Jeet Kune Do have been put forth over the years since the time of Bruce Lee's passing, many of which still exist today. The following are those I consider to be the most fundamental misperceptions (I've written about these in-depth in other articles, so I won't go into them here):

- *JKD was Bruce Lee's "very personal expression in martial art" therefore only he could do it*

- *JKD cannot be taught*

- *JKD is mere eclecticism – it's about taking the 'best' from all different martial arts*

- *JKD died when Bruce Lee died*

- *JKD's evolution and growth ended when Bruce Lee passed away*

- *JKD is simply modified Wing Chun Gung Fu*

- *JKD is simply MMA*

This article is not about finger-pointing or playing the blame-game, both of which are a waste of time and energy and do absolutely nothing to fix the situation. The villains I am talking about that exist in the JKD world today are not so much individuals or groups, but rather such things as confusion, ambiguity, apathy, mediocrity, and lack of direction.

Before we proceed any further, we need to understand first and foremost that, regardless of what anyone may think or say, there is no universally accepted definition of what "Jeet Kune Do" actually is. Some people define it as Bruce Lee's "personal martial expression." Others refer to it as the martial art and philosophy of Bruce Lee. Some consider it simply a concept or an idea, while others view it as a method of martial art research and investigation. Some use the name to refer to only the exact physical techniques that Bruce Lee used and taught, while others use it as an umbrella term to cover a "do-whatever-the-hell-you-want" approach to martial art training.

At one time JKD had a clear-cut and definite sense of identity. Its design, purpose and goals were specific and unambiguous (freedom from styles and systems, totality in combat, self-expression, scientific street-fighting, etc.). All of these things stemmed from Bruce Lee's vision regarding the art and the trajectory of that vision. However, somewhere along the way JKD seems to have lost that clear sense of identity. Over the years it has become blurred and, in some cases, completely obscured. How did this identity crisis come about? The following are some of the factors that I feel played a prominent part in it:

Lack of "Vision"

By lack of vision I am talking about a clear-cut and compelling vision regarding JKD which would serve as a catalyst to drive the art forward and give it momentum, energy, and a clear sense of direction. An example of such a vision would be something like -- "To make JKD the most innovative, cutting-edge martial art on the planet." There was no such vision concerning JKD's continued growth and development. Initially this was quite understandable because (a) nobody was expecting or ready for Bruce Lee's death and (b) no one was quite sure which direction to take with regard developing or perpetuating the art following Lee's demise. I remember how devastated Sifu Dan Inosanto was when it happened. He wasn't even sure he wanted to continue teaching JKD anymore (we should all be thankful that he decided to carry on). And in the years that followed when Dan was questioned about the direction he felt JKD should go his basic response was that he wanted JKD to "be known by many but practiced by few." While this sentiment is nice, it's not what would be called a compelling vision. This is not an indictment against Sifu Inosanto, because I firmly believe that his attitude towards the growth and development of JKD stemmed in large part from a promise he says that he made to Bruce Lee about not commercializing the art and making a lot of money off of it; a promise he steadfastly remained true. Had he wanted to, Dan Inosanto could have become a millionaire many times over by capitalizing on his friendship and affiliation with Lee.

Fragmentation of the JKD Family

While he was alive, Bruce Lee served as an extremely strong gravitational field that held the people who were training with him tightly together. After his death that gravitational field remained strong for several years, but eventually, over time, it began to weaken, and a fragmentation of the JKD clan began to take place.

For instance, some of the senior students who had trained with Bruce and Dan Inosanto at the Los Angeles Chinatown school and then in Dan's backyard gym began turning up less and less to train after the Filipino Kali Academy was opened in Torrance, California. Eventually some of them stopped coming completely. Part of this may have been due to the normal twists and turns that take place in people's lives. However, part of it was also due to the fact that there were differing and conflicting opinions over the direction JKD should go and what should be done with the art. Some people believed the art should be shared with members of the public while others felt that it should be kept small and taught only privately in backyards or garages. Some people believed that other elements and training methodology could and should brought into what was being taught, while others objected and firmly believed that the art was complete as is and nothing needed to or should be added.

Eventually, different factions or camps (JKD Concepts, Original JKD, and other splinter groups) came into existence. As with the world of religion, the question asked became "What JKD denomination are you?" To make matters worse, illegitimate JKD schools and instructors began popping up both in the U.S. and various other countries around the world.

It should be noted that over the years two JKD organizations were formed by the JKD clan to help sort out the situation, deal with the phony JKD groups, and hopefully bring the various legitimate groups together in some form of harmony and interaction. The first was "The JKD Society" which was formed in the early 1980's and the second was "The Jun Fan JKD Nucleus" which began in the mid 1990's. Senior first-generation JKD people such as Dan Inosanto, Richard Bustillo, Daniel Lee, Ted Wong, and Jerry Poteet were part of both groups (although Dan Inosanto elected to not be a part of the Nucleus following its initial meeting). I, along with several other second-generation instructors was also part of both organizations. While both organizations were armed with noble intentions, for reasons that would take far longer to explain than I have time for in this article, both groups ultimately failed in their proposed objectives and were ultimately disbanded. With various groups and people now vying for the top spot in the JKD world and staking their claim that their JKD was the 'real' or 'true' JKD, the fragmentation continued and Jeet Kune Do eventually became one of the biggest political hornet's nests in martial art history.

It's now 2020, and while many in the JKD world still like to continue to speak about JKD in terms of "family," "tribe," "clan," and other totally inclusive "we're all in this together" type of euphemisms, in reality such is not the case. As in the world of business, everyone, to use the phrase, wants a piece of the action. Some groups, while having different ideas and opinions, choose to respect each other get along amicably with one another. Others have not, choosing instead to disseminate negative material about their supposed rivals and striving to spread dissension and create discord. The unfortunate victims of such actions are the members of the public who are sincerely interested in seeking to learn about the art.

Decline of JKD Culture

When the first public training facilities at which JKD was taught (The Filipino Kali Academy, The Inosanto Academy, and The IMB Academy) initially began they all possessed what I call a strong JKD culture. By culture I am referring to the core beliefs and values of the schools, and patterns of behavior of those who trained at them. The essential nature of JKD was the same at all of the places. Simplicity, directness and non-classicalism were the foundation stones upon which the entire art was built. Speed, power, adaptability, and flow were fundamental principles upon which physical techniques and actions were developed. Sparring was the lifeblood of the art, and everything was pressure-tested out on the floor to see if it was functional and worked in a real-life combative situation. If it did it was kept, if it didn't work or work well it was tossed out.

In addition, regardless whatever other arts might have been shown or explored at the school during both the senior JKD class and the regular Phase 1-4 classes (who, even though they might often doing the same techniques that the JKD class was doing, were told they were not learning JKD but Jun Fan Gung Fu), the overarching idea was that if one chose to absorb something, it was adapted and synthesized into one's core structure so that what you ended up with was a single, cohesive art that covered all elements of fighting. It wasn't about accumulation or adding things because they looked cool or simply for the sake of adding. While one of the fundamental tenets of JKD may have been constant growth, it was growth which maintained a central theme, which was total combat efficiency. Things that were brought in were analyzed, stripped down to their essence, and simplified, if necessary, to make them more efficient or effective. This is what is commonly referred to as the "JKD mindset,"

and it was an integral and essential part of one's personal development. Even the Filipino martial arts of Kali and Escrima which at the time were being taught concurrently with the JKD were heavily influenced by this JKD culture and mindset.

In the early 1980's things began to change and the perspective began to shift. Various different arts were brought in from the outside and added to the school curriculum (as opposed to elements of them being absorbed into overall structure as I mentioned).

Although the Jun Fan Martial Arts Phase classes and Filipino Kali/Escrima were still on the menu, the curriculum now offered became more of a multi-brand experience with different arts being taught and students taking their pick of what classes they wanted to attend. Perhaps instead of training in Jun Fan they wanted to study Boxe Francaise –Savate or train in Thai Boxing or Silat. Perhaps they wanted to train in several arts at the same time. The choice was theirs. The result of this was that there was a gradual shift in perspective regarding martial art training. The mindset began to change, and as it did the JKD culture which was so strong and prevalent earlier slowly began to wane.

There is also another factor which I believe contributed to the loss of JKD culture at many martial art training facilities and has played a significant role in JKD's current identity crisis, and that is the martial art "industry." Over the years, some individuals and groups in the JKD world started following an agenda set by the martial art industry – an industry that by and large did not share JKD's goals, mindset, or attitude (remember that JKD was developed by a martial art rebel, and was rebellious in nature, throwing away anything considered non-essential to martial art training, including such things as colored belts, traditional uniforms, forms, etc.).They latched on to and began following guidelines given out by professional martial arts business consulting organizations on how to run their school and program and make JKD fit into the mainstream martial art industry so they could cater to more people. There were even programs advertising how a martial art school could add JKD to their current curriculum (regardless of whatever other arts they taught) in order to generate more income.

I personally feel that a lot of the schools and instructors who became ensnared in this trap ended up sacrificing the soul of Jeet Kune Do for profit and paying little more than lip-service to the art. And again, who paid the price? That's right, the public. How would the unknowledgeable person interested in possibly studying JKD who is scrolling through the internet looking for schools in his or her area or who walks into a school or training facility to check it out tell the difference? They had no reason to suspect that the school displaying Bruce Lee's JKD symbol amidst several others in their advertising or on their window or school t-shirt didn't actually "teach" JKD per se, or was merely using the name to cover a 'do-what-you-want' approach to teaching.

The "Classicalization" of JKD

Since the mid to late 1990's there has been a kind of movement underway, the goal of which appears to be an attempt to formalize, and in some ways even "classicalize," Jeet Kune Do. This includes such things as the addition of more and more Chinese jargon which has been steadily creeping in and now fills many people's JKD vernacular -- the development of various pre-arranged sets and forms -- the handing out of belts and sashes, etc. In more recent years some people have put a great deal of energy in trying to somehow reconnect JKD to Wing Chun in some way. Some have even put forth the notion that in order for a person to truly understand JKD, it is necessary for them to study Wing Chun Gung Fu in depth.

While some Chinese terminology has always been a part of JKD (I use some of it myself), it was always quite limited. Now one finds more and more of it being brought into full use and pushed on people for everything related to JKD, from the names of tools one uses (jeong = palm), to the names of various techniques one uses (o'ou chuie = hooking fist), to one's level or standing in the JKD family hierarchy (Si Bak, etc.), and even the term used for your teacher's spouse (Si Mo).

I'd like to address the issue of pre-arranged sets and forms, because more of them have been popping up in many people's JKD curriculum, especially since the mid-1980's (such as the "Ung Moon" form and "JKD wooden dummy sets"). When I first began training in JKD, I learned a pre-arranged sequence of kicking actions which was called "The JKD Kicking Set," which for all intents and purposes was basically a form. This kicking set was also taught in the Los Angeles Chinatown school as part of the curriculum. (You can find it listed in the "12 Week Lesson Plan for JKD") However, as soon as I learned the set I was told by Dan that I should toss it away and instead shadowbox and freelance my kicking. Years later I was also with Dan when he put together what he referred to as the "JKD Wooden Dummy Set." While this was a pre-designed set of movements, it was very fluid and mobile and built around actions that we actually used in JKD as compared to the traditional 108 movement form taught in Wing Chun. And as with the kicking set, once I had learned it, Dan told me to use my imagination and simply freelance my actions on the dummy instead. That was it as far as any forms or sets went. (For further information about this subject I suggest you read Dan Inosanto's Inside Kung Fu article *"Was Bruce Lee Anti-Form?"* which, while being somewhat ambiguous, discusses the subject in greater detail).

One of the fundamental reasons many people have been attracted to training in the art of JKD has always been the idea that they didn't have to deal with such things as belts, uniforms, and learning various martial art forms -- the very things that some JKD schools and instructors are now busy adding in. Personally, while I cannot say what the purpose or motive behind this movement to classicalize JKD might be or what those involved hope to achieve, I do, however, know it has definitely contributed to JKD's identity crisis.

Confusion between JKD and MMA

A lot of people today tend to confuse JKD with what is now referred to as "Mixed Martial Arts" and it's easy to understand the reason for this. JKD is considered by many to be the "original mixed martial art" because it seeks totality in personal combat considering all ranges and aspects of fighting. However, while there are some similarities that do exist between Jeet Kune Do and mixed martial arts, they're not the same thing. While MMA may have adopted some of the principles that exist in JKD, such as being a well-rounded fighter who is able to function in the various ranges and aspects of fighting, there are some major differences between the two. On the most fundamental level there are rules in MMA. It's a competitive combat "sport," and as such, the rules and regulations dictate the direction of training. There are, for example, numerous actions that are considered "fouls" in MMA competition that are exactly the type of action a JKD practitioner might use in a self-defense situation, such as kicking the knee, kicking, punching or grabbing the groin, pulling the hair, poking the eyes, finger locks, etc. Remember, JKD has always been about combat "as it is", without any rules or restrictions. This in no way denigrates MMA or its practitioners. Some of the best martial artists in the world today are involved in the sport, and there are many world champion MMA fighters who cite Bruce Lee as their source of inspiration. A number of them have even studied aspects of JKD to supplement their training. Anderson Silva, for example, has visited Dan Inosanto on at least one occasion to train with him at his school.

Now that we've looked at some of the factors which have played a part in Jeet Kune Do's identity crisis, the questions that need to addressed and answered are (a) What can be done to correct JKD's identity crisis? (b) How can each of us (JKD practitioners and teachers) be part of the solution to the problem? If we want Jeet Kune Do to take its rightful place in the pantheon of martial arts, there are several things that I believe we need to do:

Establish/Re-establish the vision regarding JKD

If we don't have a clear-cut vision of JKD, how can we expect other people to? We need to establish (or re-establish) a clear, unambiguous vision of what JKD is and know how we want the art to be perceived by the rest of the martial arts world. Such a vision will give us a clear sense of purpose and serve as a catalyst to drive JKD forward and give it energy and a focused sense of direction.

How can we go about establishing the vision? To do this we need to understand the thinking processes of the art's originator (the evolution of Bruce Lee's thinking). We also need to look at the trajectory of the original vision, which traveled from the objective of creating the ultimate fighting system, to the idea of doing away with martial art styles and systems entirely and offering total physical, mental, and spiritual freedom for the individual practitioner.

It's not about trying to create an entirely new vision regarding JKD, but rather to shine a light on the spirit that's already there – that's always been there. It's not about clinging to the founder (which, for some people means they need to stop staring at the 'finger' and instead look at 'the heavenly glory'). Rather, it's about understanding what the soul of JKD is – what its core values and beliefs are – what it stands for. Once the vision for JKD is established, we can kick into action to actualize it and bring it to life.

Cultivate a Strong JKD Culture

We need to make sure that the essential nature of JKD, its "DNA," if you will, is being transmitted and imparted to the new generations of practitioners coming in. In order to do that we must make sure to develop and maintain a strong JKD culture in any and all schools and training facilities at which the art is taught. As I said, by culture I'm talking about core beliefs and values, and patterns of behavior.

Wherever JKD is being taught, be it a professional martial art school, a backyard gym, or a garage, it should be a learning environment in which a student can immerse themselves and experience JKD with all their senses, develop what is referred to in JKD as the "educated eye" and the "discerning mind," and perhaps most important of all, cultivate the "JKD mindset."

Cultivating a strong JKD Culture is not about creating some brand-new sort of culture or being a slave to an old one. We want the heritage but don't want to be stuck in the past. We want the art to move forward. It's about making sure that the culture that played such an important role in JKD's development is maintained and doesn't simply disappear.

Maintain Jeet Kune Do's Relevance

The word "relevant" is defined as *"Appropriate to the current time, period or circumstances; of contemporary interest."* As I stated at the beginning of this article, there are some people in the martial art world who feel that JKD has become or is becoming irrelevant or obsolete. I disagree. While times may have changed, we, as human beings, haven't, and the fundamental principles of JKD are just as relevant today as they were fifty years ago.

However, in some ways JKD has definitely suffered from neglect in the area of its relevance and vitality in today's martial arts world. The reason for this is not because of the art itself, but because of the mindset of some of the practitioners and teachers. These people adamantly refuse to expand their thinking and step out of their comfort zone, and hold firm to the belief that if Bruce Lee didn't say it, write it, or do it, then it cannot be called JKD. They have, in effect, solidified and 'crystallized' JKD.

With the advent of mixed martial arts there has been a shift in the collective consciousness of martial arts practitioners. As a result, the differentiation between JKD and many other martial arts has been slowly but steadily eroding over the years. Some of the other martial arts have caught up with JKD technically (and I would even go so far as to say that in some they may have even surpassed it in certain aspects). And while there may be an established "core," if the art does not remain alive and dynamic and continue to develop and grow, it will stagnate and eventually glide downwards.

There is a quote that states, *"The relevant can, if we are not careful, become the irrelevant."* We need to invest time and energy in JKD to make sure that the art retains its relevance and vitality. We must be willing to expand our thinking and step out of our comfort zone. We need to remain open to progress, to changes and improvements in such things as training methods, technology, etc. But we also need to remember that with regard to JKD, growth and development isn't simply an eclectic, do-whatever-the-hell-you-want approach to training. We need to know where we want to get to and use the fundamental principles that are an integral part of JKD as guides or signposts for our journey.

Build Bridges

As I said, there are various factions and camps that exist in the JKD world today, all pushing their own point of view regarding the art. If we wish to help JKD regain its true identity, we need to strive to build bridges that unite or connect people rather than barriers that separate them; bridges that lead to better understanding and better relationships within the JKD community. How do we go about doing this? The answer is by focusing on inclusion rather than exclusion. We do it by seeking out similarities rather than differences, by finding commonalities of thought and ideas – by setting aside creative or philosophical differences and engaging and talking with individuals who don't agree with us on various subjects concerning the art. We do it by inviting people to share in an aggregate vision as opposed to a single forced vision regarding JKD.

The best in any industry bring out the best in one another, and it's no different for Jeet Kune Do. Through inclusion we can bring out the best in one another. We need to stop feeling fearful of or being threatened by other people who might be teaching JKD near us or competing with us in some way, and instead collaborate and share information and knowledge. In today's world you can go on the internet and Google anything and everything you want to know right now about anything, including JKD. So why not just get on with things and find some great people and share or collaborate with them?

Mark Twain once wrote, *"Reports of my death are greatly exaggerated."* I'd like to apply the same quote to JKD. Some people have made comments such as "JKD died with Bruce Lee" and "JKD is dying." I disagree; JKD is not dead, and it's not dying. It has become too big and too well-known for that to happen. JKD's demise hardly appears imminent -- the art has still got a lot of life in it. It's surviving, but I don't believe its flourishing. I also believe that if nothing is done to remedy JKD's current identity crisis it could end up languishing in the netherworld of mediocrity, a fate which I personally believe would be far worse than death.

Will restoring JKD's true identity be easy? I don't think so. It will take time and effort. But I choose to remain upbeat about the situation, because I believe that there are a lot of talented and passionate people in the world who believe in JKD and are just waiting for the opportunity to help restore it to its original glory, so to speak.

While it may be impossible to project the future of JKD, what is important is that we be certain JKD will be a part of the future. If JKD is to have a clear identity that identity will come from us, the people who love the art and who want the rest of the world to know what it really is. It won't come from looking to any single organization or association. We are the ones who put the heart and soul in Jeet Kune Do.

So, let's stop looking backward and saying things like, "I wish this or that happened with JKD" and "I wish someone would have done this about the art." The past is gone and no longer matters. It's all about what happens now and what happens tomorrow. Instead, let's create the future we want for JKD.

JEET KUNE DO / **NOTES**

JEET KUNE DO / **NOTES**

JEET KUNE DO / **NOTES**

www.ingramcontent.com/pod-product-compliance
Lightning Source LLC
Chambersburg PA
CBHW080724300426
44114CB00019B/2481